THE
VIRGIN
MONOLOGUES

'It may be that this does not paint the whole picture of your single life, but guaranteed there will be plenty of shared experience, hurts, accidents and adventures within these pages. With refreshing honesty, courage and humour Carrie publicly has the conversation so many of us have had in private. Her passion for Christ is a constant theme throughout this engaging, challenging and inspiring read.'

Katharine Welby-Roberts
A21 ambassador, blogger, speaker

'*The Virgin Monologues* opens up much-needed space for dialogue in the Christian community about the way we communicate to women and girls about sex. Carrie's sincerity and openness about her personal experiences offer a relatable alternative to the dysfunction of the corporate media's version of today's sexual narrative and the too often shaming response from the religious communities. *The Virgin Monologues* should be a staple in every spiritual library.'

Ben Decker
Marketing & PR consultant, social activist,
human rights advocate

'I love this book. It is honest, funny, challenging and inspiring. Just like its author. Carrie is not afraid to say it as she sees it, and whether you agree with her or not, what comes across more than anything else is her infectious passion for

Jesus and her longing for others to encounter him and be changed.'

Bill Cahusac
24-7 Prayer GB Leadership Team

'It's tough being a single Christian girl in a world full of feelings and emotions and expectations and hopes and dreams and aspirations. Like a best friend spilling her deepest thoughts onto the page – some heartbreaking and some hilarious – Carrie takes us on a journey past shame and heartache and faux pas to healing and freedom and truth. This book will be a companion to any sassy young woman wanting to make sense of who she is in the midst of all of life's stuff.'

Chine Mbubaegbu
Head of Media and Communications Evangelical Alliance, author of Am I Beautiful?

'If, like me, you're dissatisfied with the rubbish about love, life and relationships that you sometimes inhale, here's your chance to breathe in beautiful and wild words of wisdom that lead to life. Carrie has captured the art of celebrating who she is while still believing the best is yet to come. It makes for a captivating read and an even more infectious life!'

Rachel Gardner
Founder of the Romance Academy, President of the Girls Brigade

'*The Virgin Monologues* is a wonderfully courageous ride through love and life. I found Carrie's honest communication about what it's like to navigate the joyous and sometimes perilous journey through relationships refreshing. In her book Carrie has invited us to not only do better in relationships but to be a better people. I know this book may seem, on the surface, to be geared towards women. However, men will find it fascinating and challenging and will probably be better men for reading it. A must-read!'

Gabe Valenzuela
Second Year Overseer, Bethel School of Supernatural Ministry

'In this book Carrie reminds us that what is most important is actually understanding and living out of a place of knowing who we are in Christ, and how that needs to be at the foundation of how we see ourselves. When we do, it will transform how we do relationships – single people or married.'

Nici Cahusac
Wife, mother and leader

THE VIRGIN MONOLOGUES

Confessions of a Christian girl in a twenty-first-century world

Carrie Lloyd

Authentic

First published 2014 by Authentic Media Limited,
52 Presley Way, Crownhill, Milton Keynes, MK8 0ES.
authenticmedia.co.uk

British Library Cataloguing in Publication Data
A catalogue record for this book is available from the British Library.
ISBN 978-1-86024-929-7   978-1-78078-243-0 (e-book)

Cover design by Rachel Cloyne, Pickled Ink
Printed and bound in China

For the two who gave me a curious mind
and a teachable heart:

Revd May Elizabeth Lloyd

and

the late Revd Dr John Antony Lloyd

CONTENTS

Contents

Contents

Contents

Contents

INTRODUCTION

I was a virgin.
I was an atheist.
I was religious.
I was a philophobe.
I was anorexic.
I was a perfectionist.
I was full of justice fight.
I was a victim.
I was a player of my imagination.
I was a wrecker of my imagination.
I watched porn.
I was provocative.
I was confused.
I was a dancer.
I was a performer.
I was a producer.
I loved the camera – when it loved me.
I was a good friend.

Introduction

I was a bad girlfriend.
I improved after every break-up.
I was orphaned in thinking.
I was opinionated.
I was untrusting.
I was dishonest.
I was too honest.
I was the honey to his sourness.
I was poison to his milk.
I was a coward.
I was a feminist.
I was a happy singleton and a miserable lover.
I was a journalist – but not publicly.
I was a fashionista.
I was a philanthropist.
I was a scientist.
I was defined by my Manolo Blahniks.
I drank from Satan's well when I didn't love me.
I feared mankind.
I feared myself.

But I am not defined by labels. And neither are you. We could add to the list above a thousand-fold, but all you need to know is that I still wanted to make it right. For within every soul, within every mind that graces the planet, there is a moral compass that at some point switches on and wants to, above all, make it right. Whatever 'it' may be.

Introduction

I had questions. So many questions: Can we change? Why are we really here? Why can't we see that love rotates the planet, not money?

Why do some people with crippled backgrounds achieve the impossible, while others with stable childhoods sabotage every relationship they embark on?

Why are more Christian men teaching me methods of hypocrisy than men who have as much interest in Christ as I do in football?

Why can't many Christians do relationships well?

Why is there as much infidelity in the local church as there are cohabiting couples in my media circle?

Why can some marriages manage to work through the death of a child while others can't work through disagreements about money?

Why has it been harder for me to find a connection with God after delving into a sexual lifestyle?

Why was God hounding me at all?

Can we ever get past the question 'So what don't you do?' as Christians?

Can we stop dividing the world into two – believers and unbelievers – thinking we have one-upmanship because we have found salvation? Can we actually have some humility that just allows us to love everyone equally, showing honour at every corner turned?

This is not a book that argues the 23-degree angle to which the planet tilts, nor indeed who or what tipped it to that angle. We won't look at quantum physics or my neo-Darwinism fascination. I'm more interested in love than science and so we're not going to argue that one eradicates the other. We're going to look at love. Why else would I believe in God?

'If we could physically take God out of the churches in the world, 70 per cent wouldn't notice,' I used to shout. Why? Because religion removed the very intimacy God longed to enjoy with us, resulting in loveless doctrines and a Christless gospel. I didn't care about Sunday notices or whether the back-seat Bettys were arguing in choral society; I just wanted someone to tell me what made Christ's heartbeat rise and what made it fall. For no one has loved so well, not before and not since. So, if any of us are seeking inspiration in the twenty-first century, I'm seeking the most Christ-like today. And so I travelled. I travelled thousands of miles, from London to the west coast and east coast of the US, to find as much inspiration as I could.

I also posted on my blog, Her Glass Slipper,[1] an article called 'Goliath's Gonads', which held the tag line 'Would all the strong men please stand up?'

My inbox filled up with the usual messages from girls asking questions about everything from porn addiction to 'How long do I fight for him?' But then one man's response caused me to stop in my cyber tracks: 'At first I was offended being a male Christian, seeing that you assume there are no strong men in the church any more, but then I read on. Ever thought about writing a book?' From that email Malcolm Down and I began a conversation; he later became my publisher.

My life journey found me counselling teenagers in pregnancy crisis right through to training leaders in corporations on stress management. From shadowing overtly accomplished family therapists in marriage counselling to research upon research discovering how we love well *outside* of marriage.

Dating seemed to be a minefield of disasters for many of my friends, and none of us were given weaponry or advice on how to survive crossing the field to victory. Especially if we were Christians. Even when marriage was accomplished, friends were divorcing by the time they reached the age of 30, just as others were marrying for the first time – some for the wrong reasons. No one really teaches us how to do healthy relationships, what to fight for and what to give up on. What to understand about ourselves before we look for a teammate. How to be strong and happily single without an unhealthy need for a man's affirmation – yet ensuring we don't become so self-reliant that we can't accept love when it's blatantly in front of our face.

I learnt that the only way I could do healthy relationships was by watching those who had healthy relationships. These are people who could turn around the cycle of dysfunctional family and win the fight in the name of self-love.

Introduction

Dating becomes even harder if you are a Christian trying to be understood while holding moral values that match that of Queen Victoria. In the past, delightful men outside of the church have intrigued me, but of course they didn't want to wait for marriage for sex. I compromised too much to access love, and left relationships only sometimes the wiser.

I had to search for answers myself, as very few people within the church were able to share their own lessons – honestly. I wanted to collate everyone's thoughts and bring them together.

Truth is, *The Virgin Monologues* was birthed for female freedom. To explain grace one more time, so that we truly learn again that grace is the 'highest standard'. It requires a righteousness that loves above shame, a love that melts the iron cladding of religion hoping we never make the same mistake twice. Oh how God loves us. He has loved people through their affairs, to the bottom of every Jack Daniel's bottle, through their credit card maximum, to their purging need to fit into society, through their performance for acceptance, to their erotic pleasures with a man they don't even know the last name of. This isn't another self-esteem guide; this is finding God in every relationship you have, so you can really understand what love looks like. The side effect is that you will love yourself more, because you see how radically he loves you. Grace is a beautiful thing, but we've been taking advantage by repetitive mistakes, adhering to only bite-size parts of the Bible, not the entire scope of Scripture.

In grace comes freedom, comes insight, comes change. Growth doesn't repeat itself; instead, growth comes from the beautiful well of humility.

Within these pages are the trials and errors of self-experiments. With boys, with identity, with men, with relationships. Although the errors will often be my own, the mistakes of others are not to disrespect the unnamed boys I talk about, they are purely examples of what lessons we learnt – as we're all expected to make mistakes from time to time. The pages are filled with tools that might change a perspective, a relationship and an attitude towards self.

Every person who sought advice from me has helped contribute to this book: the readers of Her Glass Slipper, Twitter followers, friends, acquaintances and my own mentors. I've also added a glossary – any excuse to discuss Jared Leto* in more detail (* = refer to glossary).

If this book was given as a gift to you and you don't know how you feel about God, that's OK. It's important to question, it's important to find yourself within the reasoning or possibility of the phenomenon. I would never have fallen in love with God if I hadn't been an atheist (and an angry one at that) beforehand. So I get it. It didn't need to happen, but my journey helped a new apologetic perspective.

Introduction

If I could ask for anything it's this: don't be prejudiced against a person who believes in God. Even if they've royally screwed up – they're as flawed as the rest of them. Don't use blanket statements without doing your research outside of a couple of Louis Theroux documentaries based on Westboro Baptist Church or the Taliban. That's not God, that's religion. God seeks to love in abundance. And the book focuses on how we therefore love each other. So suspend pre-judgement and fear of the word 'Christ'. He's not the dentist. Christianity is a sound doctrine. If you take away what imperfect people have tried to show you before, something new may be revealed to you. It's rare. Despite 2.5 billion (a third of the globe) Christians walking the earth, it's not easy to find real Christ-like love within a dating culture. But it isn't out of reach.

Just as the disciples wrote their eyewitness accounts of walking with Christ in the Bible, I'm writing eyewitness accounts of Christ-like people – to encourage and enlighten you that loving well does still exist in the twenty-first century, despite internet trolling, paparazzi-infested hatred and success being elevated as a more important thing than being kind.

If we understand that God is love, the rest of this book should be an entertaining yet hopefully engaging read, at the cost of my own pride, but then again, you are worth it. Whoever you are.

So put the kettle on, or open a nice bottle of Chianti, open your heart, kick off your Converse or your Choos, and airplane mode your iPhone, because I trust that, with your attention, my pain (joyful or triumphant) will be your gain.

Father – the master of creation and master of love – you have all of me, all of my mess is yours, use it for good. Use it to empower her, for even though I don't know her name, I care for her heart. And, as I make many mistakes, may self-discipline be seen as a freedom, not a chain. May she apply her own life to the stories, may they be relevant. As she encourages men once more, may they apply their humility, and may she find strength to lead a movement of stronger women.

Be our ecstasy, be our everything, be the light in the dark and protect us all from debilitating scepticism and from judgement. Introduce each woman to her original design, without lies, without chaos, but instead with revelation or eureka moments.

Thanks Papa, for always answering prayers, even if it wasn't within our desired timing. You've not failed me yet.

So, for the record, as you read these monologues know that you were meant to be here, just where you are, reading this book, introducing you to yourself, over and over again, until you find your representation of love in relationship is finally manifesting.

With light, peace and stiletto-hugging love,

Carrie x

PART I

THE G(OD) SPOT

The pursuit of men chasing your coat tails may be enchanting, but the pursuit of knowing yourself as a daughter of God is the key to how you receive and how you give love. The greatest of commandments is to love your neighbour as you love yourself. Self-help books might pick at the surface, but nothing will shift, until a greater power than you melts your pride. As God lives in you, you must love yourself in order to truly love God. Self-criticism, the misunderstanding of who we are, misaligns the placement God is meant to have in us – the core of the self. We cannot be a prize candidate for a teammate if we haven't done any work on ourselves and our perspectives – digging deeper into the ultimate being that created us. The closer you are to him, the closer you are to your true identity. It cannot be in any other order. Your identity needs to stop living in reaction to a past and instead start living in response to his voice.

I

THE 'WHY' FACTOR

> 'The Bible tells us Jesus Christ came to do three things.
> He came to have my past forgiven, you get a purpose for
> living and a home in heaven.'
>
> (Rick Warren)

'I'm afraid if you and Dad thought I could become a third-generation minister, you may need to reconsider me as your daughter.' This was a confession I made to my mother in our vestry, aged 6. As if I was born purely from a ministry production line.

'Why do you say that darling?' my mother asked, ensuring nobody else was present.

'Have you ever seen Billy Graham wear armbands when he baptizes people? No.'

This was a fair argument for a girl who had only, up to this point, seen people (who, unlike me, were able to swim)

3

being dunked underwater in our neck-deep baptismal pool. I naturally thought my father was trying to drown people with their own authorization – a sort of public euthanasia, so to speak. No one thought to tell this infant what was going on most Sunday mornings, so monologues would run through my tiny brain: 'Oh no – don't worry about me, I'll just watch you shout about this big leather book while you stop people breathing, getting everyone soaking wet, Mum standing guard with beach towels singing "Shine, Jesus Shine". Meanwhile, I, your only child, assume you're just a little aggressive with new members of our church. My word, no wonder you're paid minimum wage. You could have chosen interior design or computer programming. But no.'

When asked who my parents were, my response was usually, 'They professionally half-drown people, then sing about how wonderful it is. An odd career choice I grant you, but they seem happy in who they are.'

Somewhere between hunting wildebeest and selling hand-stitched crafts on eBay what we *do* has now defined who were *are*.

You see, I thought everyone's identity was wrapped up in their career. A concept completely off the beaten holy grail, but a mistake I would continue to make into my late twenties. Oh alright – thirties.

Let me explain: somewhere between hunting wildebeest and selling hand-stitched crafts on eBay, what we *do* has now defined who we *are*. Our worthiness has become measured by Mercedes McLarens and Alexander McQueen*. Elements that are never mentioned in someone's eulogy.

Before you hop on the career love cart and assume this might be Rick Warren's *Purpose Driven Life – Part 2*, you're mistaken. There is a difference between purpose and career. And too often, even after Warren's bestseller, we've been victims of the modern vacuum that starts every conversation in networking circles with 'So what do you do?'

For a decade I worried too much about money. I believed that if I didn't achieve some acknowledgement then I'd be rendered useless. Sacrificing my childhood dreams of becoming a Teenage Mignon Mutant Turtle, or whatever they were called, I began journeying through different jobs, including dressing as a giant Mr Kipling cake (promo girl), working as a direct marketer for publishing titles such as *Practical Fishkeeping* and *Land Rover Owner Magazine*, a casting director's assistant, a video editor, creative director's assistant, advertising producer, pregnancy crisis counsellor, sex ed. counsellor, life coach/soft skills trainer, careers advisor (the irony), actress/retail assistant, a Black Thunder Babe* for local radio, head of new business for digital advertising . . . The list erupts in volcanic motion until I hit a place where I heard God say to me:

Carrie, what are the desires of your heart?

So I wrote them down. Writing is my go-to for anything meaningful; the epicentre of where I could talk with my heart without my silly brain interrupting. But all I kept jotting down were things I wanted to achieve: freedom with money, influence to shift unhealthy mindsets, family, friends, problem solving, that Mercedes McLaren, a rustic home and bathroom large enough to fit a chaise longue in.

Did I answer his question? Not remotely.

For another few years I sprinted along the wind of London's rhythm, believing I had to keep up with the modern era of expectation, earning enough to keep up an apartment overlooking Tower Bridge by doing jobs I didn't feel called to. With a pinch of charm, anyone could be a producer, anyone could organize call sheets and collate the best team to shoot a commercial for Red Bull. When could I put the real me into my career?

Two redundancies forced some reflection. Breaking from the 'it's not enough' eighty-hour-week mentality, detaching from answering that wretched, 'What do you do?' I was reminded, through eating humble crumble, that all we are ever required to do is love well.

That's it. One word – love.

Relationship suddenly rated over rental payments.

Nothing hit me so hard as when, years ago, I stepped into one of the most beautiful mansions I'd ever stayed in, overlooking Beverly Hills, asking a successful friend who owned it, 'Are you happy?'

Emmys and Oscars littering his shelves, he stared over the land: 'I'd like to share it with someone. This means nothing without people, without relationship, without family, without love.'

'Well I love my boyfriend, Carrie, but who's going to pay for the beef stroganoff I'm cooking him?' I know . . . and I hear you.

Don't discard responsibility. The greater the calling, the greater the responsibility. Just don't mix it up like cake batter with your identity. Because jobs change, but your soul remains. Bringing you to your job is more vital than what the job will bring to you. Note the order.

In a humbling conversation, Bill Johnson, the senior pastor from Bethel Church, relayed to me: 'Your purpose is your 'why'. Without your 'why' there is no purpose.'

If your 'why' is that round of applause, the raised eyebrows of guests, the sunken cocktail bar in your condominium, your 'why' isn't worth dying for.

If your 'why' is that round of applause, the raised eyebrows of guests, the sunken cocktail bar in your condominium, your 'why' isn't worth dying for. You'll be too chicken to die – in case you lose it all. Your 'why' must be bigger than material, bigger than yourself, bigger than humankind.

I never wanted a job I wasn't passionate about. Until I discovered what that job was, I panicked over pennies, believing I *had* to run around the car park with a video camera, filming boys dressed up as old women on modified mobility scooters with embedded Xbox consoles. I fell into jobs as easily as I fell in love, hoping I would discover who I was once I found the correct career or relationship.

But I still hadn't answered his question:

What are the desires of your heart?

Due to my seasonal deafness to God's voice, he decided to make it stark-ravingly obvious. My boss, the creative director of an ad agency, found some of my writing and, passing my desk, dropped my words in front of me nonchalantly suggesting: 'You should write.' This, from a man who found it much easier to throw a chair at you than a compliment, so his words ran deep.

Then Dawn, a friend and successful writer herself, casually plonked into conversation: 'You should write, babe,' encouraging me to get braver in my expression of faith versus religion. It was the only activity I did where I didn't watch the clock, staying up until the early hours piecing together sentences, words, idioms, until my heart rested. When I cracked a sentence it was divine intervention and I could get shut-eye.

In Latin *De* means 'of' while *sire* means 'father'. I noted that the desires in my heart came from my heavenly Father. I had ignored them for a decade. My desire for Vivienne Westwood Red Label created an ignorance that suffocated a dream that he had for me. My money matters and lack of trust in his provision held back the passion he had stitched into me. Then this year, I found a photograph of me, aged 5, smiling behind a plastic typewriter, with my dad looking over me, beaming.

It was in you all along. I designed you to be at the end of my quill.

What if I'm not enough? What about that massive pay cut? What about the comments made by horrid trolls online? All this ran through my head continually, until a particular comment appeared online:

'Come on guys, Jesus doesn't exist. We all know that Shakesphere [sic] wrote the Bible.'

I needed that spoonful of sugar. Bursting into a thousand hysterical chuckles, I was hauled out of my self-indulgent rut.

Was I not aware that I would get persecuted for having a faith, especially if I wrote about it? Was it not a wish in me to apologize for the poor efforts of the church in recent decades, and yet, make sure people didn't give up on the body of Christ entirely? If I didn't attach my value to God's assignment, and just saw it for what it was, then why was I timorous about getting on with it?

I signed up. If fear was the hurdle, then it could go and do one. Because if God sacrificed his Son for me, I should use my MacBook Air for him, not for myself. He had now become my 'why'.

You're covered. Be still. Write with me.

The mess I brought into this discovery felt embarrassing. The constant chasing for self-security that I had undertaken meant that things hadn't felt good between him and me. But he had resolved within that entire decade of mishaps, trials and sampling of careers to get me to a place where I now had a thousand stories ready to use in my writing.

Like a placebo, he worked around some of my surprising Mr Kipling cake-promotional-girl choices, all the time wishing I would just check in to who I was in him.

There are too many of us who are career types these days. You know what I mean: ruthless in relationships; self-righteous in pecuniary focus. Working midnight till midnight, striving for a fulfilment that rarely arrives after that pay cheque, the Lion award, the bonus, the accolade. Only in our honest humility do we surrender to that 'why'. Anything else is futile. Anything else just doesn't satisfy.

When I started listening to the desires of my heart, suddenly there was something I was willing to die for, enough for me to want to live. Something to represent. Herein lay my 'why' and herein lay my serenity.

God doesn't want to rewrite your past – he will help you use what you learnt back then in the present, and he celebrates all the small victories when you choose to overcome, when you battle down the trenches and discover more of yourself through a major trial.

The 'Why' Factor

Discovering God was the only way for me to discover myself. For you, too, your job, your role, your status, what you are known for, doesn't define you. The apostle Paul butchered Christians with heartless celebration, until his career path changed in that God encounter. Only grace made it possible to twist his life story and motivate him to write letters that produced a third of the New Testament. It came with a servant heart and an overflow of God's abundant *amore*.

> **It's not a matter of Adam and Eve; it's a matter of you – for no one has been designed the same as you.**

So get ready. Change the tune. Dig deep into the heart that was designed by him. Ignore the unreasonable expectations.

It's not a matter of Adam and Eve; it's a matter of you – for no one has been designed the same as you.

But if your 'why' is about you, your purpose will not reach past your doormat. If your 'why' comes out of your love for him, it will stretch to the ends of the earth.

II

DADDY'S GIRL

I have been misrepresented by those who don't know me.
John 8:41–44
I am not distant and angry, but am the complete
expression of love.
1 John 4:16
And it is my desire to lavish my love on you.
1 John 3:1
Simply because you are my child and I am your Father.
1 John 3:1
I offer you more than your earthly father ever could.
Matthew 7:11 (From 'The Father's Love Letter', Barry Adams)

Those were the days. When Dad was at gunpoint on the inner German border shouting over my screams to my mother, 'Get Carrie out of here!' (I was 4 years old.)

No matter what circumstance I faced with my rather adventurous, Bible-smuggling parents, I never assumed for a minute that we'd be harmed – Gamma gun to the temple or not. Oh sure, in the moment, no one likes to see a lethal weapon with which in one slip of an angry soldier's finger your dad could be shot. Up until this point everyone had been so nice to me.

Dads are responsible for introducing us to our identity, but, when things go a little awry, we need to get hold of the how-to tools to ensure we can still excel as women – no negative dad-talk holding us back.

But no shots were fired. Dad charmed his way out of the situation, just as I expected he would. My trust and joy in my parents meant my childhood was magical, heavenly in spontaneity, and I had them all to myself.

I had eighteen years of a joy-led father and five years of an emotionally distraught one. Dads are responsible for introducing us to our identity, but, when things go a little awry, we need to get hold of the how-to tools to ensure we can still excel as women – no negative dad-talk holding us back. The only remedy I've found to have a 100 per cent success rate is when our heavenly Father comforts us over our earthly father's mistakes.

My dad was brilliantly breathtaking. The man impressed me, loved outrageously and fought ferociously for justice. He introduced me to an adventure-filled life of creating biker clubs for the runaways in the roughest estates in Manchester, building up church communities, heading non-profit organizations and fundraising millions for the outcasts (lepers), sheltering the rejects (the elderly/homeless) and listening to the fractured (schizophrenics).

Often I witnessed my dad fight for me as a girl, when I was too young to protect myself, too young to understand my own value: 'If you so much as breathe on my daughter, or threaten to flush her head down the school toilet one more time, I will hunt you and your ear lobes down. I will drag you to your parents, if you're not already feral boys living in forests, and I will annihilate you with one blow of my tongue . . . in Christian love of course.'

This is an example of the 'love' delivered by my dad to two boys at my school who picked on the girl who had Baptist ministers for parents (me, aged 8). Dad was 6 ft 4 in and I made a decent shield out of his right leg, as he read all 4 ft of them their rights: 'Are we all completely clear on the regulations moving forward?'

Heads down and a mumbled 'Yes'.

My dad's terrifying authority quickly changed to: 'Great! Come on kid.' He snuggled my head under his arm walking away, 'Let's get you on that Ducati to brush off this escapade . . . do that walk you do, Carrie.'

'What are you talking about?'

14

'You know, your strut walk that says "My dad's got my back".'

'That's not a walk. There is no such walk.'

'You're doing it now! That's it!'

'This is my regular walk, Dad. This is how I walk.'

'That's my girl! But slow down, my leg is bad from shrapnel in the Second World War.'

'Dad, you don't have a bad leg, nor were you in the Second World War.'

'How would you know? You weren't even born.'

'Yes and neither were you. Stop it, stop limping.'

Our conversation faded out as we walked further away from the village bullies accompanied by my father's asthmatic laughter. But when I hit 18, Dad had an operation on his heart so severe that it changed all of our lives forever.

He came out a very different person to the one who went in, barely surviving the bypass. A touch of brain damage from too high a dose of morphine took away his capacity to have control in certain areas of his life and behaviour. He began to sterilize his life with alcohol after a doctor suggested he should 'take a couple of sherries before bedtime' to help his insomniatic suffering. The doctor wasn't to know it would turn into a disruptive bi-weekly habit that slowly became a regular walk down misery lane.

Overnight my father, the man who had taken ecstatic joy in a risk-taking life, became unable to protect me from his own inner fear-ridden dialogue.

15

The roles had reversed as Dad clung onto my leg, saying, 'I'm not well, Carrie. I'm not well.' I'd cry into him and Mum would find us often in a heap on the floor. Other days I'd be angry, having little compassion for addiction. I wanted to fix it all and fight for him, after everything he had done for me. The mix of emotions went from bitterness to deep sadness, from hope after six months of sobriety to despair within his relapses.

Driving to a London party in 2003, I received a phone call in which I was dealt the news that Dad had died in his sleep that afternoon. I was 23. He was 61. By the time I returned, he had already been removed in a body bag and police had already interviewed my mother.

I stared at his coffin, numb, as a white butterfly flew out of the flowers sitting on top, up into the steeple of the church. That white butterfly would become a powerful symbol for me two years later.

No matter what our dads were, what they turned into, whether they left or whether they're still faithfully around, comfortable in their family home, wearing pyjamas while constantly hitting themselves with spoons for entertainment, 'father wounds' are the words thrown around in the couch-surfing of therapy rooms. We've seen the flummoxed individuals who've worked on their parental mishaps every lunch break for the last thirty years and still they're a little 'deranged'. Watching people live in reaction to their past gave me little hope. Until I met a few women who had suffered rape, abuse and abandonment but were still able to embrace the word *daughter,* this time within the essence of a much more powerful Papa.

'Oh here we go – then the heavenly Father swept in and filled in all the little earthly daddy issues with a giant air hug, saving the day as a whirlpool of cherubim and seraphim adorned her apartment with tulip petals and Kate Spade* handbags.'

You're incorrect. But you were close.

We might joke about the countless orphan/daughtership/sonship books on the shelves, but only a few are digesting the point. I'm sick to my back canines of watching women try and lead men, keeping up the walls of mistrust, self-sabotaging a decent date night just because the men couldn't read their minds. Expecting them to emulate the same kind of fight a man would make in a covenant marriage, when they've only been dating for three months.

I was not immune to orphan thinking. If anyone hurt me years ago, when I was yet to understand the difference between orphan thinking (I assumed this referred to Battersea Dogs Home and the fate of a German Shepherd) and daughters, I would shut them out, maybe shout a little, and seek to move on to the next man, without so much as a Kit Kat break.

If we're Freudian about this, you could connect the dots; see that my dad's relationship with the Black Dog and his ability to hide vodka bottles in the spare car tyre would have built up a few 'trust' issues. And it did. The man I would have stood in front of a bullet for became a shadow of his former Jekyll self, and it echoed clearly in the relationships I had with an actor/alcoholic and consecutive needy/drip-like chaps that didn't value themselves.

When dads stop pouring value into you, or tragedy makes you feel abandoned, you question the value they once introduced you to, which can lead to relationships full of nothing but hurt-filled reaction.

Orphan thinking anyone? Not as appealing now is it? The urge to get revenge, the fight for that last line with a girlfriend who consistently cracks on to your boyfriend, or the boyfriend who consistently cracks on to your mother, is all umbrella'd under the orphan anorak. Because we don't believe there is anyone out there fighting for us. There is no stillness in the workings of an orphan brain.

Orphans are insecure; daughters have credence. Orphans compete with their own children; daughters are everyone's cheerleader.

I took the reins. I called the shots. I determined how competitive I would be. I manipulated every man (fluttered eyelashes) from the valet guy, to film directors. My need for success was a little too important when I failed. I didn't see favour as a blessing – just the results of my own hard work.

It got pretty exhausting. I burnt out from striving, more than twice. When things didn't work out with my plans for my career, I blamed no one but myself. Another excellent approach to healthy mindsets. (It isn't.)

Orphans are insecure; daughters have credence. Orphans compete with their own children; daughters are everyone's cheerleader. Orphans operate with a life of narcissism; daughters focus on opportunities for others as well as themselves. Orphans get jealous over their own friends becoming your friend; daughters love their worlds to collide. Orphans serve God to earn the Father's love; daughters already know they're loved so serve from a sense of divine acceptance. Orphans are scared to risk; daughters jump regardless. Orphans seek comfort from material possessions and appearances; daughters are focused on the ethereal. Orphans – you get my point.

I turned atheist for a few years, and the world became monochrome. I was independent, with a penchant for cutting people off if they were not kind. I was angry and I was determined to prove the non-existence of God through scientific argument. Science, however, couldn't discuss why I needed to love and be loved. So I kept being haunted by Christ. And oh how he loved me in my ignorance. I dabbled in Buddhism until I stepped on a snail and was worried it might have been Dad. Then tried Islam, Quakerism, everything. Until God's pursuing got the better of me and I saw a son and father relationship of beautiful royalty in concept and reality: Jesus and his Father. I sighed as I closed my eyes in the garden one afternoon, and said inwardly:

'I give up trying to give you up, God.'

I felt something on my nose, opened my eyes and there she flew, the white butterfly. The same breed that, two years prior, had flown from the flowers on my father's coffin.

I'm here. I'm yours. I always have been. I'm so happy you've come back to me. I want nothing and no one else to have you. For I created you. You are my daughter.

There he was. My perfect, ever the romantic Father; the fighter to the end. Graciously giving me free will, but never giving up on my return.

I know I'm not the only daughter who has experienced this: 'God said to me: "Even though you don't like me very much, and you don't trust me as much, will you let me take the position of Father in your life?" My reply was: "I don't like you, but I have seen the enemy, I know that way of life. I could stay that way or I could choose you, and I think you're better. I don't actually like you, but I'm choosing to trust you. I choose to trust you because I do know you're the better choice." It broke something spiritually.'[2]

God is free will. And we can all decide on a belief. But embracing him as a father? There's your disco. There's your intimacy. There's your personal relationship, a relationship that will make you want to love others as your siblings, love yourself as a daughter and love your Father in any way to make him happy. There's your answer to identity. Belief is one thing – love in a father is the punch line.

Jesus Christ is still to this day the only documented human being that walked the earth without exhibiting any flaws. Considered to be one of the greatest thinkers the world has ever known by non-believers, as far as I'm aware his wisdom didn't come from an early manuscript of *Men Are from Mars and Women Are from Venus*. His relationship with his

God is free will. And we can all decide on a belief. But embracing him as a father? There's your disco. There's your intimacy.

Father (not the high-brow God we often religiously revert to) is the reason he was able to bounce Lazarus back from having no pulse, walk on H_2O, tell thunderstorms to pipe down and predict who would betray him before Judas ever kissed him goodnight.

Then, there in the gruelling six hours of the crucifixion, where Jesus struggled up and down to find a less painful way to exhale, a Son asked his Father to forgive the very orphans who were gambling over his clothing as his earthly mother helplessly watched on.

The reminder renders me breathless. I'm shocked that I had the audacity to think I was god-like in opinion, that

I was entitled to constant apologies, that I had every right to shove people out and cut them off because of their misbehaviour, that I had a right to do whatever I wanted to do 'as long as no one gets hurt' – the orphan tag line for an ignorant and arrogant short-lived win.

If you enter a church and the image of the cross isn't moving you, you're not close enough to him. You're not understanding the bond of fathers and sons, fathers and daughters. You're not getting the whole point of Christ at all. You're not a daddy's girl.

A healthy fear for the Lord creates a humility that begins to open up a heart that's been walled for too long. Sometimes that only happens when a woman has faced enough emotional leverage to actually want to change – it's what happened to me.

I didn't know what daughters looked like, until I began to ask what made certain women tick: women who found it hard to get offended; women who didn't need to have a reason before they obeyed the Lord; women who heard from the Father in the first place.

These are daughters. Hunt them down. Watch them diligently and, as you learn to be a daughter, you will naturally gain spiritual fathers who will remind you again of your worth. Your circumstances need not dissuade you from an even greater Father, from his detailed and intentional love:

'Even if mothers forget, I'd never forget you – never. Look, I've written your names on the back of my hands. The walls you're rebuilding are never out of my sight. Your builders are faster than your wreckers' (Isaiah 49:15, *The Message*).

You'll know if a sense of daughterhood is rubbing off onto you because you'll begin to have brave communication without falling apart. You'll love people in their mess, without cutting them off. You'll make room for another opinion. You'll make room for people full stop (within boundaries). You'll work from a place of overflow in love, rather than from a vat of lack. You'll love your earthly father and forgive him for his imperfections.

Today, I love my dad and I hold no resentment towards those last few years where he needed my love and my mother's more than ever before.

Daughtership isn't an excuse to regress back into the foetal position while watching *Bambi* on repeat. It's actually a doctrine that will help you to embrace the true meaning of identity in Christ so that you can love others fully, without the unhealthy emotional displacement of past papa hurts.

This is the pinnacle to your identity: no daughter, no discipleship.

You'll know if a sense of daughterhood is rubbing off onto you because you'll begin to have brave communication without falling apart. You'll make room for another opinion. You'll make room for people full stop.

Your heavenly Father is the one who waits for you to sleep to give you prophetic dreams. The one who'd never let anything happen to you that you couldn't handle. The one who brings serenity when you're tearing your curtains from the pain of grief. The one who gives you divine wisdom in a moment of red-blooded madness. The one who introduces you to your identity, so much so that stress becomes like putty in your hands and criticism is nothing but comedy material. He's the one who has been waiting for you all your life – so that he can walk before you.

If we gave our Father three uninterrupted minutes to come and love us the way he really wanted to . . . we'd never turn back to what we knew before.

III

THE CURSE OF EVE

'She senses the worth of her work,
is in no hurry to call it quits for the day . . .
She's quick to assist anyone in need,
reaches out to help the poor . . .
Charm can mislead and beauty soon fades.
The woman to be admired and praised
is the woman who lives in the Fear-of-God.'
(Taken from Proverbs 31, *The Message*)

When I was 7, I 'married' my next-door neighbour. Simon was his name. My attire was quite something: a neon Nike tracksuit and a pastel headband that attached a Care Bear pillowcase (my veil) to my head. The witnesses were Sam, my wind-up musical teddy bear and Gobo Fraggle, from The Muppets' *Fraggle Rock* circa 1987 (Simon insisted that the guest list would be lopsided if Gobo couldn't attend).

It was a small ceremony, led by his sister; she needed us to hurry up so she didn't miss a very important episode of *Alvin and the Chipmunks*. After the 'I dos' I grimaced when he tried to kiss the bride and suggested we instead build a hospital made out of Lego. Our marriage was brief. Three hours to be precise, before I asked Bugs Bunny to annul it. He complied, Simon didn't. It got messy and Sam and Gobo ended up being our divorce lawyers.

Until the man of her dreams has materialized with some diamond attached that shines brighter than Galadriel from *Lord of the Rings*, she'll flick through *InStyle* until her fingers bleed.

Infant fantasy aside, it did make me wonder: from an early age in our female psyche, do we always desire to be the Eve to the Adams of the world? To be the helpers, the *ezer kenegdos*? Are we so distracted with finding the husband and/or having children that our very journey in life is bypassed until this point and the unique design God created us to be outside of marriage and children is entirely misplaced? In short, are we waiting for Adam to save the day when we should know we are saved already?

26

The Curse of Eve

This is the curse of Eve – thinking that we're nothing more than a spare rib designed to help a suitor. The curse of Eve says, 'Everything will be redeemed once I have found my husband. Once I've seen his face my heart will settle to its expected BPM and I will be happier and, possibly, less insane.' Eve says, 'You were made for him and nothing else.' Eve says, 'You were formed to procreate for the human race.' So, until then, until the man of her dreams has materialized with some diamond attached that shines brighter than Galadriel from *Lord of the Rings*, she'll flick through *InStyle* until her fingers bleed, making mood boards based on what eye colour she thinks her future husband will have.

As Rosalyn Sussman Yalow, Nobel Peace Prize-winning medical physicist, says: 'We still live in a world in which a significant fraction of people, including women, believe that a woman belongs and wants to belong exclusively in the home.'[3]

That yearning for Adam or his sperm can distract her present joy as a single woman. Instead Eve manipulates any situation or relationship in order to get her fix, ignoring entirely God's (possibly opposing) plan for her.

I'm in my early thirties, not married and have no children. Not yet. Do I begin to panic, as a female, that I'm not wedded to Adam and therefore think that God's design for me has been put on the shelf because I let centuries of social expectations dictate who I am? Or do I trust in God's plan and listen to his voice today?

If Adam is running as fast as I am towards Christ and we fall in love while crossing paths, then great. But I'm not waiting for Adam. We've both got jobs to do. I am a spiritual mother now. Our purpose is still manifesting in the same way – we are both to be a helper, a servant to whoever crosses our path. As Bill Johnson explains: 'God made me to be a contributor to society through servanthood to excellency, whereby I live in the reward of a heavenly favour. Rewards with meaningful relationships . . . Anytime you have humanity without Christ at the centre – you have a violation of design.'[4]

This is not an anti-mamma campaign or a 'let's burn our Elle Macpherson bras' feminist manifesto. I'm the first one crying in jubilation down the hospital hallways when my friends give birth – especially when I observe children being born into strong, emotionally wise marriages, with parents who were solid in their identity before they were even married.

And this is my point.

We are not our children, we are not our jobs and we are not the husbands we marry. We are individuals that have been uniquely designed to serve a world and bring other people freedom. No one is excluded.

I've heard women declare that our only reason to be on the earth is to procreate. Would they honestly say that to my mother's face? She attempted to have children for thirteen years, and was terrified to hold a child in case she kidnapped it. I was the only one of her pregnancies that made it to full term. What if she had never had me? What would they say to women who've never met their Adam? What about the women who have had all their children, but their Adam decided to leave after having an affair?

If we see our identity as merely Eve the helper we limit ourselves to either the experience of life in relationship or a psychological breakdown, should Adam want to call it a day.

To cut our purpose to just two purposes: 'helper' and 'bun warmer' makes things a little limited; it also limits the ambitions or potential for our children should we ever have them. As my friend, Claire Heydon, explains: 'Having my own identity teaches my children by example what it means to lead a fulfilled and purposeful life. You do no justice to God's plans for your life if you surrender your life to someone else's. He said he has plans for YOU. Some women are scared to be bold and live their lives, so they

Cristina Fernandez de Kirchner, Aung San Suu Kyi and Angela Merkel all did a little bit more than help Adam with his crossword puzzle.

hide behind a busy mask of "helper" instead of taking the risk (and hard work) to pursue their dreams. In my personal experience, I am a better mother when I am fulfilled personally.'[5]

For those who've not met Adam, or can't have children, you can still be the *ezer kenegdo* without them. Saint Teresa mothered more people than any other woman I know. If Emmeline Pankhurst* hadn't refused to be a 'household machine', hiring help for her and her husband, who else would have led the suffragettes with such force? Cristina Fernandez de Kirchner,* Aung San Suu Kyi* and Angela Merkel all did a little bit more than help Adam with his crossword puzzle. They led governments, won Nobel Peace Prizes and ended up under house arrest while fighting for a nation's children – not just their own.

> **To the women who've not yet met their Adam; to the women who 'had it all' and 'lost it all' too: please take your place in the world because we need you.**

To the women who can't have children; to the women who've not yet met their Adam; to the women who 'had it all' and 'lost it all' too: please take your place in the world because we need you. There is something in you that no one else can do and you will be attacked by lies of inadequacy, lies of worthlessness to unremittingly ensure you don't go out and fight the good fight. Build up a fortress of love around yourself and towards others, stabbing the spirit of comparison as you walk upright.

The Curse of Eve

Don't begrudge mothers of motherhood; and mothers, don't begrudge women who are destined for a purpose outside of children. Be the real feminists, not the feminist writers online who moan about each other; become a union to enforce powerful and influential Eves across the planet. For, after all, Adam blamed Eve for a mistake they both made.

If Eve was so influential in the fall of humankind, then she can be influential in the rise of it once more.

IV

LOVING THE HELL
OUT OF YOU

'Comparison is the death of joy.'

(Mark Twain)

When you consider restocking your refrigerator with copious amounts of meat because Lady Gaga just walked down the red carpet for the Grammys in a dress made of venison, you know the world has gone a little, well, gaga for celebrity idolatry.

I worked in a top ad agency that would bust its clever thumbs to tell you, the consumer, what to buy, when to buy it and how to feel when you did buy it. Creatives were paid huge amounts of money to be the greatest manipulators on the planet. And boy, were they good at it. I'd watch my favourite art director walk out of his office after five hours of brainstorming with a stockpile of paper thrown into bin bags: 'More of my genius work,' he'd tell me, sliding back into his office for another five hours.

Advertising has been noted as being one of the most influential world changers to date.

Alone, it has changed history: how we function, how we interact in relationships, how we view ourselves, forever. Manipulating the spirit of comparison became more lucrative for the ad men on Madison Avenue, and more deathly for the consumer.

As the ad world saw how

Advertisers pretended they were introducing you to a better version of yourself, but actually they were really introducing you to the latest craze.

much money could be made by dictating, subtly, which products to endorse, what brand to wear, which personality to duplicate, you lost yourself. I lost myself. We all lost ourselves. If just for one ten-second television interval. For some, a lifetime. Advertisers pretended they were introducing you to a better version of yourself, but actually they were really introducing you to the latest craze.

There you were thinking it stops at your washing detergent. The cultures we live in, whether the swinging sixties or the new romantics, attempt to emulate trends that make us feel good, that keep us 'alive'.

But it never lasts, does it? The Atkins diet faded as quickly as your Justin Timberlake crush. The comparison of lifestyles, bodies, cars and success imploded to such an extent that half of the world's population now struggles with relationships, work and fulfilment. It is all down to one 'small' problem. Comparison. A made-up distortion that was warmed up by the steaming lava of hell.

Are my sentiments a tad strong? Let's see shall we?

Commercials cost more to make per second than feature films, and for a good reason. There are powerful people, with a lot of money, who understand how to make music, a good tag line, a cute animal, a witty quip, or a nicely cinematographed car, persuade you to run to your purse and click online, so you can be just . . . like . . . her.

Whether it's sucking in your gut with Spanx*, manoeuvring in ankle-breaking platforms, cutting out aspartame-ridden chewing gum, taking those excruciatingly embarrassing selfies, rapping a personal rant on video social networks or standing in a queue of 50,000 other wannabe *X Factor* contestants – in order to be like 'her', we are officially exhausting ourselves.

Whatever happened to original thought? Whatever happened to relaxing into who we were meant to be? How do I ever get the chance to discover what I stand for, if I can't walk to work without digital posters following my steps on the London Tube shouting at me what perfume to wear, or what man I should fall in love with?

The world is getting sharper and more manipulative, studying patterns of your own specific intrinsic behaviour as you casually browse (without a care about your identity) the internet.

But here's the rub. It's not what you focus on, it's *who* you focus on.

So I turned to Christ. He might have worn the Armani of seamless robes in his time, but it didn't define him. He appreciated the join of a well-sculpted oak table, but he didn't seek to sign his name on it. He gave his life away, and therefore retained

> **Here's the rub. It's not what you focus on, it's *who* you focus on.**

a million more lives – becoming the most powerful life that ever lived.

So stop looking left, stop looking right. It's the blueprint he made of *you* that he's interested in – not the person you are trying to be. No identity can be sincere if we're copycatting the person sitting next to us. Although God created the Miu Mius* of this generation, we mustn't define our worth or happiness by trying to be like them.

Outside of heaven, this dimension is full of trickery; so don't let hell invade you by telling you you're meant to be someone else.

You need to crack open the fabrications, shedding a little light on the misnomers of today's falsities. You might as well kiss goodbye to tomorrow if you can't wave hello to yourself today. Because those who tell you what you should be will change their own minds next week. It's not constant, and it's not what the body was made for. The very people who influenced you are not easily influenced – how do you think they found their voice in the first place?

The common denominator among all the creatives my boss hired was that they owned who they were, and never apologized for it. Yes, sometimes they needed to be reined in. Yes, it's the most decadent industry out there. But perhaps we could learn a lesson from their self-confidence?

The paradox is that finding the real you is simply a decision. To turn down the volume of messages that ring in your ears, to give up your belief that behaviours, self-image and even religious doctrine define your identity – then go and ask God. Why are you 'shoulding'* yourself based on unreliable sources?

It's time to turn to the only book that breathes life. And I don't mean this one.

Ask him now. 'God – how do you see me? What am I to you? Why was I even created?' If you don't get an answer, ask again. Note the first words that come to your sanctified mind. Then pin them on your wall. Do this again the next day, and the next, until you have a list of descriptions. You'll discover that the only entity that has the authority to tell you who you are has defined you clearly. If the answer is negative, you're listening to the wrong voice. Tell it to shut up. Then ask again. Ask until you're moved to tears in answers. I don't care how many episodes of silence this takes.

Some answers will be hidden on purpose, just so you dig deeper into understanding who God is, to bring you closer. Some things will not be louder than your radio, because he finds more intimacy in whispers.

If comparison lives in you, and you're aware you're doing it, then it's time to find your weapon and shoot it, point-blank – dead.

You won't know the strength of his affirmation until you see the strength of the opposition. If you give your heart to contradiction, if you fuel questions about yourself and give them authority, you will continue to live all the negative things that you've given yourself permission to think about yourself. So what are you going to give life to and what are you going to kill? Because if comparison lives in you, and you're aware you're doing it, then it's time to find your weapon and shoot it, point-blank – dead.

The first temptation on this planet was not met by biting into the apple, it was met by questioning what God had said. The result was that we suffered arrows of disconnection in relationship, shame, self-condemnation and dishonour.

Romans 12:2 says, 'Don't become so well-adjusted to your culture that you fit into it without even thinking. Instead, fix your attention on God. You'll be changed from the inside out' (*The Message*).

Nothing else will transform your mind forever like God can. Nothing is as solid, as consistent, as loyal, as unconditional, as sacrificial, as sincere, as genuine, as beautiful as him. It's why regularly reading the word of God is so important to our identity.

The greatest curse of this generation is self-gratification, puffed up in the guise of 'self-love'.

Once you know what he thinks of you, the next step is to give up your life. Give it up. The greatest curse of this generation is self-gratification, puffed up in the guise of 'self-love'. Own who you are in the creation of God, but don't keep it to yourself.

This is the beautiful tension: I find people who love the hell out of themselves, by loving the hell out of each other. Their lifestyle practises love without pretending, without performance, without comparison.

You can only carry the presence of God if you've let go of carrying your own anxiety. Yes, embrace who you are because you are a creation of God, but omit the blasphemous shoulds in your mind so you can become powerful in administering heaven's agenda above your own.

Loving the Hell Out of You

Oh sure, wear a dress stitched with filet mignon, so long as you're doing it from a joyful God-filled desire, not a need to reflect someone else or a need to perform for attention/affection/false love.

Once you have embraced who you are, and learned to give up your life to God, you'll influence the influential, men will trust your opinion about yourself and you will walk out of your own office with another stockpile of genius ideas. You'll overflow with more and more and more.

Unlike Lady Gaga's dress, you want your heart to be tender, to be nurtured in love not shoulds, not envy. So don't question what God has said about you. Question why you were choosing to listen to someone else, when the true identity of who you are was in you all along.

V

ANTHROPOPHOBIA

'For am I now seeking the approval of man, or of God? Or
am I trying to please man? If I were still trying to please
man, I would not be a servant of Christ.'
(Galatians 1:10, ESV)

'I've been blocked by two women. One of them was
@carriegracey. But I don't care, she was a bolshy
b**** anyway.'

The temptation to reply, 'Such poetry. Is that Byron
or Keats?' was great, but I refrained, reminding myself
that (blocking sexually inappropriate public online
comments aside) my time wasted on such a response
could be better spent: picking out morning eye-gloop,
spending a while asking why I had found a bit of hum-
mus on my right calf, finding that remaining lost Uno
card.

But it's been quite a journey to this nonchalant dreamland and sometimes, even now, I need some alignment.

Winning votes for house captain, or owning the most coveted sticker collection in the playgrounds of Cambridgeshire, really does scupper one's ability to be humble. My popularity thermometer became my 'worthyometer'. In earlier years I had faced bullies who had contempt for my faith. Now I was in high school, becoming popular had taken too much governance, and I wouldn't notice what effect that had until later. I didn't get arrogant, I got people-pleasing. My drug in my teens and twenties was injecting myself with other people's affections.

> **Owning the most coveted sticker collection in the playgrounds of Cambridgeshire, really does scupper one's ability to be humble.**

Shocking, isn't it? Such an inner wiring developed and I forgot how to be me. I was chameleon-like, spreading myself thinly to all groups at school. I 'did right' by everyone I knew. Disharmony made me shudder. Criticism cut my heart. When I heard a peer describe my solo recital of 'Memory' by Andrew Lloyd Webber as 'a sound akin to someone drowning' I didn't sing for another fifteen years. I wonder to this day whether that critical girl ever worked out who the 'moustached high-pitched man' was

Fear of others is one of those thumb prints in life that wrecks identity. It's human nature to seek validation for what we do, who we are and what we say.
But there's a capped quota on others' opinions.

at the back, shouting during the school nativity play as she performed Mother Mary: 'You may dress like the mother of Christ but the similarity ends there!' (If you're reading this, I'm sorry. I'm sorry I did that to you.)

Fear of others is one of those thumbprints in life that wrecks identity. It's human nature to seek validation for what we do, who we are and what we say. But there's a capped quota on others' opinions. To be defiant against what people think is surely just contemptuous and arrogant? Surely these non-people-pleasers are nothing but thick-skinned, egomaniacs missing a sensitivity chip, ruthless in business and even more so with people's feelings.

Not so fast, sailor.

Some people are as callous as Tony Montana*, but people-pleasers (hear me out) can be as fraudulent as the egomaniac, for they both feed off the same source – society's opinion. Neither care for love, just self-love and, more often than not, self-medicate on it for dysfunctional kicks.

In church we are bulldozed with the messages of loving each other as you love yourself, turning the other cheek and laying down your life for the church, but somewhere in that we get as confused as an octopus curtseying to the queen. We override God's approval for that of a stranger. Doing so is the equivalent of attempting to lay a spirit level on a moving slug. It's just not reliable. It won't be consistent; it's a pointless measurement.

This inner wish to have people love us and us love them is an essential part of our make-up, but when we burn out, when we compromise our own selves beyond

If Christ had rested on the *approval* of humankind, there would be no New Testament, no Christianity.

what we are capable of, when we cry into our soup because the ex-boyfriend has turned everyone against us to avoid him looking bad, here is when the fear of others really has to disintegrate into glitter. Remind yourself of your worth to the only entity that ever remains consistent, outside of time and space, the very creator of your own DNA.

If Christ had rested on the *approval* of humankind, there would be no New Testament, no Christianity. His identity was secure, which was why he could argue well, yet be unoffended, why he could love amongst disagreement and why he could dine with the ugliest of souls.

Writing articles on faith is often like a red rag to acid-high bulls. I was accused of being chemically imbalanced, weak, a non-believer in dinosaurs (my favourite) and a murderer (accurate in relation to spiders) after an article I wrote about counselling girls in pregnancy crisis, who, despite any opinion I have on their decision, I can't judge and must love. 'Repent while you can,' the email came through. 'This is exactly the reason why Christ still hangs on the cross.'

Apparently this sweet theologian wasn't good at finishing books – notably the gospels. Again, my silence fell and my justice button was diverted to Christ's face.

It can sting, yes, but here's the important key to note: 'However much worth and validity you place on other people's approval when things are good, so it will be expressed with exactly the same intensity when their approval is robbed from you. Therefore it's utterly pointless to seek your worth from good or bad press. Be it online trolls, or people you have met. What is most important to you will be what governs you. It's not whether people agree with you, it's how you love them regardless.'[6]

How your critics deliver their criticism will dictate the authenticity of its candour. After all, I want to learn, so will always listen, as long as there are no revenge tactics or self-projection. Sometimes I use the opportunity to love regardless, which confuses the hell out of them. Usually, it's just fear, self-hatred or low blood sugar levels that cause the criticism and they just need feeding. Quite like a chimpanzee.

Their disagreement with me shouldn't mean I reject them. But if my identity is wrapped up in their opinion of me, I become poor in rationale. Seeking to be right over relationship, seeking the approval of everyone in my life produces a sardonic response if they don't. Walls build up and I'm no longer accountable because it's not safe to come out. Allowing other people's reactions to dictate my day means I'm up misery creek without a speakerphone.

I learnt the perfect way to react to irrational people's displeasure from my boss when I worked in advertising. He called his creative department into the boardroom after receiving the most complaints that year for one of our national television commercials. We thought we were up for a thrashing and potential firing as our boss held a huge wodge of the letters written by TV licence payers.

Silence fell and we could barely look at him. He began to read them out. 'Listen to this. "I've never been so insulted by such an offensive advert for fitted kitchens, I felt as if I was watching domestic violence without inviting it into my living room."'

The silence continued. We waited.

He threw the letter over his shoulder and, beginning to laugh hysterically, he continued to read the next few.

'I'd rather eat lard, then vomit and then eat that, than watch this.'

'My wife has left me. I blame your commercial entirely.'

'Dear creative director, I've already called the police on you. Wherever you are, they are coming.'

'You're an a***hole. I loved that furniture store until you ruined my concept of the perfect counter top.'

The advert was of families disagreeing about washing up. As the teenager slams the door, we pull back to see they are in the middle of a furniture store, and it was all a prank. The complaints were so off-balance, that in order for the boss to change our perspective, he turned their comments into prime stand-up comedy material.

Before I could lift my head up, fifty people were crying with laughter. My boss, one of the top art directors in the world, the man who had made the company's turnover into nine-figured numbers, had no problem with criticism. Dare I say, he found it enjoyable. He loved being controversial. He couldn't look people in the eye that cared about another's opinion, but he had time for those who risked being dynamically confident in their identity.

To influence the world, you can't care what it thinks of you.

If we can't take a cheerful approach to criticism from strangers, then we sure as pandemonium are not going to be able take critique from those people in our lives whose opinion is valid – parents, leaders, friends who love you,

peers who want the best for you. You have to have accountability with those close to you. We need those people to
grow – embrace the face of honesty, I say, and don't go
crying in the corner because they've hurt your feelings. The
President couldn't do his job without this approach – you
can't reach your potential if you're so scared of their opinion. To influence the world, you can't care what it thinks
of you.

Embalming my happiness in what others say is not a
stable, not a trustworthy, not a worth-the-risk temptation.
It is as futile as eating a chocolate chip from the Cookie
Monster's hand.

Don't be the former 'naive Carrie', who used to ensure
everyone else I functioned with was safe. If you're not aware
already, that approach makes life a little sedated, with the
address book slowly becoming obsolete. Morgan Freeman
was busy, I couldn't find the email of Sister Renate, which
left my mother and she, upsettingly, only responded to 481
of my 483 emails a day, which, I thought, was sloppy.

After one too many times of letting the other person
take the power seat, I began to seek value and veracity
from God. I no longer had to have safe people around me
to feel safe: God made a home within me that felt glorious enough for me to handle most things without fear.

No matter what someone else did to me, whether it was a
man who didn't treat my heart with much consideration, a
friend who had high expectations that I couldn't physically

or emotionally meet, gossip or criticism – if I responded by going around trying to tell everyone the truth, I'd be starved of oxygen, left for dead on my front pathway, with a small chance I'd be eaten by geckos.

When does it stop for you? Not until you're eating nothing but egg whites to achieve the size zero shape your gorgeous curvaceous body was never made for? Not until you've lost all your friends because you totted up on the scorecard every present of generosity you gave them? You're thinking of heaven and you can't invade earth with it if you're spending all your breath performing for everyone.

No opinion is ever worth your own inner sanctum, for it is within there that dynamic movements are created, where great dreams flow from the heavenly think tank.

Perhaps your actions are meant to make people think, to stir things up? If I did everything to gain approval and didn't have a faith to keep me accountable, I'd have buckled to a line of cocaine in the industry.

Getting your identity direct from God will ensure there is no place too uncomfortable to walk into, no feedback too much to take. Your standard of who you are must never be determined by the body politic around you, but the concepts beyond the very macrocosm you are born into. Keep your head up, looking at canvases painted in the skies, and you'll soon realize that no opinion is ever worth your own inner sanctum, for it is in there that dynamic movements are created, where great dreams flow from the heavenly think tank, before they invade earth and, where you, once you get over yourself and get into him, shall score hearty hat-tricks for the glory of the Lord.

VI

GOD ♥ SECRETS

'Yet you desired faithfulness even in the womb;
you taught me wisdom in that secret place.'

(Psalm 51:6)

The attempts people make to seek spiritual connection have probably matched David Blaine's magical illusions. Just consider those who lie in open graves waiting for the stars to change formation, religious groups pulling out their hair strand by strand, food fasts for seventy-one days, people standing on precipices of skyscrapers ready to take their life. Each one is bartering with God to give them a sign that he's real. The search for a deeper connection with God has been an inner yearning in us since time began.

But those who carry a presence, who handle obstacles with poise and grace – that tangible 'there's something about them' substance of divinity, all have one thing in common: they pursue a renewing of the mind within an intimate relationship with God in secret. It was the secret place that made David king, it gave Gideon courage and retained Jesus' ability to keep loving amongst hellish adversity.

I spoke to Katie Veach about her own secret place. 'The secret place, my favourite place, is the place I go to connect with the one who is my everything. It is the place I direct my heart, and when I arrive there is the most wonderful exchange of love and adoration. He hands to me strength, hope, delight and encouragement, and I give to him my thankful thoughts, my honest questions, my silent dreams and my forever devotion.'[7]

The secret place holds the most intimate of conversations – the MI5 of dialogues. Christ-likeness doesn't come at the click of your OPI-manicured fingers*, downloading podcasts or reciting a good Joyce Meyer quote. Encounters are not your God. They are a bi-product of a relationship with God. Your hunger for him will determine the extent to which you lay down your heart and rest upon his magnificence. It is in that quiet place that

> **It was the secret place that made David king, it gave Gideon courage and retained Jesus' ability to keep loving amongst hellish adversity.**

you will meet revelation for those you love as much as comfort in your grief.

Even as an atheist I couldn't deny that Jesus was a heroic philosopher. His relationship with God is the intimacy I'm trying to achieve – a connection so tight that none of my thoughts are not of God. Here, the withdrawal of my own ego, self-indulgence, the laying out of mess, the exuberant gratitude, the processing of hurts, the daughter talking to her father, the servanthood of love, an outlet so raw, so unpolished made me see a brand new face of God. One that loved me sharing secrets, one that wanted me to talk candidly, with no shame to hide behind. When we do something that shows him how much we adore our own creator, the day becomes kaleidoscopic in colour.

The secret place holds the most intimate of conversations – the MI5 of dialogues.

It was only in making time for my most loyal friend that I discovered the treasure of the secret place with him. So powerful was this discovery I question how sincere my faith was before this notion was revealed to me. It didn't come through gold dust on Bibles, glory clouds at the ATM, financial breakthrough, nor legs growing longer. I learned the simple truth: he favours those who believe they need him the most.

I'll backtrack. In 2009 I took part in a three-part documentary series called *The Big Silence* for the BBC. The producers found five 'busier than Obama' people that had fast-paced momentum for their daily nutrition. Camera crews followed me during my usual week as a TV producer. Once they recorded how peace-less our lives were, St Buenos, North Wales became our temporary home: a Jesuit silent retreat that required us to live in silence for eight solid days. You read that correctly. No talking, not even at meal times, which meant I had to use improvised sign language to ask someone to pass the ketchup.

We had one hour off daily to speak with an assigned mentor. Sister Renate had a waiting list of people from around the world, desperate for her anointing in the presence of God. Her stillness shifted an atmosphere, so naturally – I wanted a crate of it. Within minutes, she recognized that I had used my busyness as a way of avoiding grieving for my father, as well as any real intimacy with the Lord.

We did everything we could to avoid the silence. Father Christopher Jamison, former Abbot of Worth Abbey, told us: 'Silence is a gateway to the soul and the soul a gateway to God.' We weren't sure . . . On the first night, three out of the five 'Obamas' planned an amateur escape to the pub, only to be busted by a rolling camera. To liven up the ambience, Jon played music from his iPod through his headphones; we all leant in for Jay-Z's musical tones, sipping the bottle of wine I had smuggled in that night. It was the quietest disco in recorded history. We caved-in the next day, sticking to our contracts, realizing that perhaps there was something in this uncomfortable silence.

With Z1 cameras hiding in the bushes, filming us like wildlife, this was my first taster of the secret place. Many critics had suggested, 'Anyone will hear from "God" when their walls are broken down, all luxuries taken away, making them vulnerable.'

My response to the criticism? Why would anyone want to live with walls? If you're ashamed of who you are, fearful you won't be loved if you show some vulnerability, by all means barricade yourself in for the one crowd. People will bungee jump off Golden Gate Bridge but they're terrified of showing their raw self. Where's the hunger for the truth?

I decided I wasn't scared of facing the hurdles to get a chance to experience him – even if it was on national television. In my hours of dedication to silence, God loved it when I shared my deepest concerns. I developed a healthier fear of the Lord, instead of questioning him to other friends: 'Just how loyal can God really be if he watched bad things that happened to me?' I realized that my tiny pea brain could never summarize the greatness or mystery of God, and that the secret place was the proper place to ask him questions, rather than diss him in public. My loyalty to him was becoming more recognizable. I knew he loved it because his presence got as thick as a dust cloud, enough to make you skip your meal, or sleep in the chapel overnight rather than your bed.

I had finally found liquid gold on tap; convents also became comprehensible to me. Forced encounters may begin a new journey, but it's not until you get smacked in the face with a four-by-two of wisdom from someone who bathes in the secret place, that you'll covet it too. You see, it may look different for everyone, but the point is, you go to your secret place before going to anyone else.

The secret place coughs up conviction, our own feelings, our own needs, and seeks to resolve them. Sometimes without noticing, disgruntlements disperse. Just by sitting with him.

Recently, while listening to Ludovico Einaudi, I fell onto the floor crying out, 'I stole money from my mother's purse when I was 7 and I'm sorry! I used it to buy Q-tips from the newsagent, and I didn't even want them.' In the depths of the solace, I heard:

What do you need?

God knew that this was not some religious conviction to flagellate myself because of a packet of cotton buds, but something else. I checked myself.

'I want to know my dad is OK. I know he's in heaven, blah blah blah, [I talk to God like this] but I need him to know that I'm sorry I didn't get to say what I wanted to say to him before he died.'

In a second I found myself at the top of a mountain, looking over a valley of winding roads, brighter than a Palm Springs day. In the distance was an object moving swiftly round the bends. Coming towards me was a giant Pan European motorbike made of platinum, and riding it was my father at his very peak on earth: tanned, sprightly, ageless, not wearing a helmet (of course). He jumped off:

'Carrie! What, has it been about five minutes?'

'Ten years, Dad.' I smiled and smashed into him. Of course with no pain and no questions, he didn't respond to the time lapse and tapped the side of the motorbike.

'Keep close to him, because you have a job to do, kid. Value the secret place as if it's your only possession.'

'The materials are very different in heaven,' he flicked it and winked at me.

Our playtime was what I missed the most. Then I told him the things I needed to say. He smiled and kept playing with my hands. Around him were another thirty people (angels?) on more platinum motorbikes. They all seemed pleased to see me.

'I need you to know, I was just your temporary father,' he told me. 'It's time to focus on the Father who can do what no man can. So keep close to him, for he's more than you and I ever dreamt of on earth. Keep close to him, because you have a job to do, kid. Value the secret place as if it's your only possession.'

He mounted his bike and said, lastly, 'And by the way, I've seen your husband.'

'You have!?'

'Yes.' He smiled. 'He's magnificent.'

'HE IS? Dad you never say that word?'

'I only use it on men who *truly* love the Lord.'

And with that, he rode off laughing, without the asthmatic edge he used to have.

Did I make it up? Sanctified imagination is spurred by God's presence within us. Those thoughts could never have been my own, for I can't teach myself about these things, or bring myself hope, or bring wisdom to a confusing circumstance. No counselling session, no maxing out of my credit card, could have bought me that exuberant sensation of closure. I woke up the next morning with a brand new heart.

Wearing your Sunday best, practising *lectio divina*, or playing a few Jesus Culture CDs might bring insight, but it may not always bring a personal rawness in relationship with him. We can hide behind it like routine rather than leaving the space just to 'be' with him and hear what he wants to say to us personally. I love tradition, but we must make sure that it does not mask that intimacy. That relationship cannot be taught, it must be hungered for. The despair in the twenty-first century is found in dysfunctional relationships, miscommunication and yet could be so easily remedied behind closed doors in simple conversations – nothing polished, no educated answers from a Henry Cloud book.

As Bill Cahusac explains, 'It's actually really simple. One, God wants to be found. He really does. He wants to spend time with us. He longs to hear what is on our hearts – sharing our hearts with him is the foundation of intimacy. As we do that he shares his with us. Two, expect him to speak to you. Three, learn to become aware of his presence, whether you feel anything or not.'[8]

As conversations with God become the paramount place of function, and you replace people-pleasing with divine connection, you'll start to believe you are the head not the tail, you are above not beneath, you are powerful not broken, you are beloved not rejected, you are comforted when you mourn and you are championed in celebration.

If you've ever had a taste of *Selah*, just like discovering Enya (sorry) for the first time, you'll want to cancel your engagements, hang up the phone, love a little harder, letting go of anything you used to forge faux comforts.

You want to know who you are? The secret isn't the place, it's seeing you as a person in the reflection of his eyes. Go talk to him. Really talk: no rehearsed script, no performed worship. Just take you, no matter how you feel, but be ready, because you've no idea what kind of platinum ride he could take you on.

CARRIE'S PRACTICAL POINTERS

- You are not your job. You are not your success. You are a daughter who has been asked to love radically while on earth. What have you always wanted to do but been too chicken to? **It's time to not let fear be your scapegoat and jump off the precipice.** The Lord will give you wings, before you need catching.

- Parents are imperfect. Surprise! Living in reaction to the mistakes of yesterday will misalign your heart for today's relationships. **The closer you are to God as a father, the more being a daughter will become second nature.**

- Adam is not the beginning of your happiness. He's an extension of it. Are you desperate to marry? To settle? Is the biological clock ticking too loudly? List what joys you have right now, without Adam. What dreams you could fulfil now? **Focus on your current season and be grateful for life.**

- **No two Eves were meant to have the same story.** So why are you comparing? Observe where you sense comparison and dismantle lies. Write down what society says, then write down a column directly next to it to tell you what God says about you.

- **Fear of man: the greatest factor stopping you from finding your identity.** Kindness has become so distorted by people-pleasing; we've placed man's approval in front of God's. Want to know if you're suffering from anthropophobia? Get someone who loves you to give you constructive criticism: an area you need to work on within your character. If you see it as a growth opportunity, then you're on the right lines. If you can't stop thinking about the comment and you respond in defence, or distance, you're getting your worth from the wrong source.

- **The secret place is not for the faint-hearted.** It requires you to get raw, get real, tear the room apart if you must to find the intimacy as you feel God's love in the very darkest corners of your mind. Nothing is too horrid for him. What happens behind closed doors is what matters most; it's where transformation actually happens.

- **The secret place is the secret to finding your real Father, but this looks different for everyone.** For me it's morning coffee and talking as if he's sitting with me. For others it's walking in nature, painting, playing. Part of this journey for you is to find your own sanctuary. It just must be something that no one else gets to be a part of.

PART II

HERE COME THE BOYS

Ah – the pursuit. The tension. The butterflies. The confusion. The bizarre things that happen which leave us sipping on a cup with our girlfriends asking, 'Huh?' The chase can occur in any given moment, but should you mould yourself around such an event? Not necessarily. Men will desire you, you may even be deemed a goddess, so you will have to work out how to steward the dating process well. But remember, wherever you lay your high heels – that's your home. The stewardship of their pursuit, the stewardship of your own heart if you like them, are the foundations of dating. Like all false starts, you have to begin the race again. And we don't want that, do we? The stronger the woman, the more still she is within herself, the more likely the men shall pursue. So get ready, look out for telltale signs that suggest a man isn't protecting or honouring your heart and learn how to handle yourselves in the chase. After all, there's only one like you in the world.

VII

YOU SAY COFFEE, I SAY COMMITMENT, LET'S CALL THE WHOLE THING OFF

'The nearer you come to relation with a person, the more necessary do tact and courtesy become.'

(Oliver Wendell Holmes)

Ladies, we've got to chill out.

A coffee is a coffee. A dinner is a dinner. It is not marriage, nor even dating unless it's stated as being. It does not mean you should begin to Photoshop your babies or emboss your love calculation in calligraphy.

You let things happen, at a halcyon pace, via a mutual decision. The speedy-uppy thing that many women (come on girls, we've all done it) can do (the dreaming, the over-expectation, the HE LOOKED INTO MY EYES FOR 2.5

SECONDS) really should be managed to a dignified, if not zero level. Because the panic alarms are going off after date two and that's the reason why men are pooping themselves about just wanting to discover someone. If they suggest a coffee, the girl has bought a prom dress for the occasion. So men are giving up. Or, if they do try, they are doing it in secret and asking girls to sign a disclaimer.

If a healthy man who seeks to honour women wants to date you, he will say so. If he doesn't, why on EARTH would you want to go wasting your cross-network minutes anyway?

When two people hang out, a lot, if they are healthy, they will have communicated between each other where they are at, be it intentional friends, poker players or non-committal make-outs with a beneficial car-pooling route. They will let you know if they are dating; just please give them room before you start creating a ton of fear from your own crazy projections and then start building expectations between two people or, indeed, unnecessary pressure.

Are many girls too needy? Do they excrete an air of desperation that not even Dettol can eradicate?

I sound harsh. Because I am, darling. (I will compliment you later, I promise.) But Carrie is getting on her Jo Malone soapbox. I'm sick of seeing boys not stepping out and asking chicks on a date – and yet I understand why they aren't. And I can't even have a conversation with some men without them assuming I am visualizing our babies while they talk about their thoughts on the recent Alan De Botton novel.

It starts with us.

If a healthy man who seeks to honour women wants to date you, he will say so. If he doesn't, why on EARTH would you want to go wasting your cross-network minutes anyway?

Let's all hold hands while we recognize the difference between expectations and expectancy. Expectations are based on pre-planned wishes; expectancy is birthed from a trust in God's plans above all. Your motivation will be obvious, on both counts.

Despite the beautiful single girls surrounding me, despite the abundance of emotionally intelligent men I've now encountered on my travels, despite the fact that my teacher in ministry school will make all the singles stand up in class to take a good look around at the potential, not many of them are dating.

Hmm. Over-excitement about coffee perhaps? IT'S A LATTE. YOU DIDN'T MAKE OUT OVER THE CIN-NAMON POWDER, DID YOU? SHEESH.

It's OK. I've slipped a sedative into my green tea. It'll kick in.

Nostalgia has thumped me and I'm reminded of those phone calls years ago from girlfriends calling at unearthly hours. This is an actual conversation I had, a conversation more real than Hoff's hair:

Friend who needs help: 'It's urgent. I got a TEXT!'

Me: 'Huh?'

'A TEXT FROM HIM!'

'Who? What? What did it say?'

'It says . . . Hi, sorry to disturb but is your friend Sarah single?'

'Oh no.'

'That classic I'm-pretending-to-be-interested-in-someone-else-but-actually-I'm-interested-in-you game.'

'No, I think he might actually want Sarah to be single – so he can date her. Maybe one day make a little love to her.'

Silence . . . then she proceeds:

'He could get her number from anyone. He chose to text me. He was thinking of me when he wrote it. Me. Me, not Sarah. Me. He put a kiss at the end of it. So that means only one thing. I should ask him out.'

'It's an absolute, not even last resort, categorical, NO from me.'

'You're right, I should ask.'

'Is this signal bad? I said NO.'

'He's good to go?'

'NO! HE PROBABLY HATES YOU, YOU FRUIT LOOP!'

'He likes fruit? I'll buy some for our first date.'

'I give up.'

'What should I wear?'

'The sweater of shame . . . Farewell. Call me from the other side.'

I know that my friend is not alone in the 'over-analytical, jump at any opportunity, must find my prince charming' category.

The 'pretend' bumping into him, the tactical reasons to communicate, the subliminal social network statuses geared to make him notice. The 2,000 online photos publically displayed of the same shot, in the club toilet mirror, of you, on your own, with no friends, with just different shades of lipstick on . . . wearing that sweater of shame.

When the man you are interested in doesn't get in touch, you blame it on wearing the wrong shade of L'Oreal. Truth is, he sensed your tension a mile away – like a shark to human blood.

When the man you are interested in doesn't get in touch, you blame it on wearing the wrong shade of L'Oreal. Truth is, he sensed your tension a mile away – like a shark to human blood.

Keep yourself protected, with a splash of wisdom and oodles of communication. Be relevant to his feelings, don't get carried away with your own and if you're even having to question whether the dude likes you, then just do yourself the dignified favour and remind yourself courting needn't be this hard, or exhausting.

It's supposed to be romantic, beautiful, outrageous and bonkers.

Believe me, sister, I've been there and I've felt freedom since I stopped this ridiculous excitement in 2005 after one too many moments of getting ahead of myself. Freedom in this makes things real.

Co-dependency starts as early as an over-hopeful coffee date.

There's nothing more beautiful than being at a random village hall event dressed as Lara Croft, to find yourself being dragged outside by a handsome man, pinned against a wall and him saying, 'OK here it is – I like you. I really like you. And I want you to be my girl.'

My response? 'Where do you think we are at?'

'This is where I think we're at' – CUE KISS.

That's when you know the dude likes you, hopefully more than for just a kiss, although stranger things have happened.

Co-dependency starts as early as an over-hopeful coffee date.

Girlfriends, let's take a stand and enjoy who we are as beautiful solos. I know why you panic, I know you want to protect your heart. But protection is different to fear. Let's not make ridiculous rules about what things are or what they mean. Let's start listening to what men actually say and note, more importantly, what they *don't* say.

You Say Coffee, I Say Commitment

Do not allow the excitement of a text message to get in the way of God's plans for you, or your Saturday night. Powerful women make powerful choices, and as you just let men be men, you can finally be you.

VIII

THE CHASE

'This morning I was awakened by that familiar whisper.
*"Carrie, there are no maybes in the Kingdom. Today you make a
decision on him. You must not let him rest on your maybe, for he
is my child, and I can't see him suffer one more day."'*

(Journal entry, 2014)

Today, we live in a world where a feminist reporter gets rape threats on Twitter for campaigning to have Jane Austen on the ten pound note, polygamy is on the rise[9] and the only time Jesus is mentioned in the news is in the search for the mystery man leaving $1,000 tips in New York. I often need to remind myself that, despite the modern trappings of human behaviour, my standards need to be created by me, by Christ's renewing of my mind and not the social network society I live in.

The Chase

Such standards include the bar I set for men who pursue me. I'm sure you've read the books *He's Just Not That Into You*, *The Rules* and Francine Rivers's *Redeeming Love*. These books reveal different variants of what it looks like for a *real* man to want you. With six billion people on the planet, there are as many stories of the man's pursuit as the number of US votes. Such is the insane creativity God writes in our life stories.

Feminists will state that we have as much right to pursue men as they do to pursue us. But, since the cave age, men were designed to hunt and gather. We were wired to watch out for threats (why don't we remember this in dating?) and I know that when I've done the chasing the men have felt emasculated, questioning later whether they really did want me. We do pursue them, but with an act of responding, rather than initiating the kill. I'm not suggesting it's illegal to pursue. It's just nice to know you don't have to question whether they wanted you in the first place.

At the age of 7, the pursuit came in the form of me playing kiss chase during lunch break. I would intentionally run slowly for a boy I liked, playing the naive card: 'OH NO, HE CAUGHT UP WITH ME!' Alternatively, I would spontaneously fall ill with 'emphysema' if there was a boy who didn't tickle my fancy. I didn't know what emphysema was, but it seemed to always bring the desired effect and get-out clause.

Once I reached adulthood, very little changed, except the hideous tap shoes I'd wear to school discos (thank you

Prada for saving me) and the locations of the chase (the playground was replaced by rooftop bars, dinner parties and Monmouth Coffee House*).

The method is still the same; the standards have risen a little higher. Firstly, I appreciate a man who's past puberty. Secondly, they don't get to kiss me quite so easily, not until we've had some conversations and I see that he's not placing me above God.

Saying no has never involved me giving fake digits or switching my rings to my wedding finger. Unless he gave me Ted Bundy vibes, which, to be honest, has been rare.

The man shows interest but I decide if I give him my number. Saying no has never involved me giving fake digits or switching my rings to my wedding finger. Unless he gave me Ted Bundy* vibes, which, to be honest, has been rare.

What if the lines are blurred and you're already friends? He hangs around you all the time, texts you most days but isn't taking the initiative to ask you out. When those conversations could steer towards the subject, he drops in the B-bomb: 'I'm like a brother to you.' Or, worse yet, 'You're like a brother to me,' seemingly not having noticed that you are a girl at all. Maybe set your standard at least for a man who can distinguish what gender you are.

The Chase

In reality you like him but you're too scared to ruin what you have in friendship by bringing the subject up. But how integral is your friendship if you're hiding something as important as your emotions from him anyway?

I've fabricated the premise of the friendship before to avoid my real feelings and to keep him close. I would say to myself, 'I'd rather have him in my life as a friend than nothing at all.' But that can only ever last so long, until he begins to date someone called Tallulah and questions why you never want to hang out with them. Or braid her hair.

I've got friends who have journals dedicated to the type of man they would like in a future spouse, rarely setting foot outside their apartment, and others who will be open minded enough to try at least one date with someone, regardless of first impressions. How the chase develops will often depend on how worthy you think you are of being chased.

From having men who sing to me from the West End stage in front of thousands, to sending written love notes or flowers to my work, I am still the one who calls the shots on how much they get to be in my life. I don't give in because they've offered me attention, my decision rides on the respect they show in different scenarios. From lessons learned, the higher the standard I set right from the beginning for myself, the better they steward me – and their intentions. We're not talking high-maintenance; we're talking standards of excellence.

There is a difference. Communication, boundaries in order to retain value, with them sharing their feelings, is of paramount importance.

Just think about expensive carpets for a moment; how you treat your hemp carpet (please take off your Choos) sets a precedent for how people treat it when they enter your house. It's the same with us. The less we value ourselves, the less valuable we tell people we are and therefore the less we raise the bar. And raise it we must. Those who keep their standard low – be it physical boundaries or allowing them to spend all their time with us without a relationship commitment – will be the girls crying about men's disrespect or self-gratification.

Is he healthy enough to pursue you? Does he ask God about you first? Does he take ownership rather than blame God for his confusing communication?

Let's be honest. Any attention is a delightful adventure for most. On a basic human level, we all look around us in the world for validation. But may I ask: are you going to let a man with a façade of performance that would impress Michael Bublé tell you you're worth the pursuit?

Or are you going to keep sticking to your core values, your understanding of yourself and your vision of what healthy relationships look like, no matter how good the banter might be?

The Chase

This is how we play this funny little game of croquet. You know you. I know me. We should know what fits us as a team and that's what I'm looking for. Romance aside – is he healthy enough to pursue you? Does he ask God about you first? Does he take ownership rather than blame God for his confusing communication? Is he able to talk with his heart? Does he show signs of fear in pursuing you? If so, he's likely to not know who he is. More importantly, therefore, does he know himself through God's eyes? If he doesn't, and he's asking everyone for their input or opinion on you, he'd ask Snoopy for advice if he stumbled across his kennel. Don't get me wrong, Snoopy had some decent ideas, but a man who has a decent history with the Lord will treat your heart with honour right from the beginning, not when he's finally in love with you and he's on cloud nine.

Proverbs 4:23, the verse that says, 'Above all else, guard your heart, for everything you do flows from it,' was written for the girl who didn't stop to think about herself before she allowed a boy to bulldoze her world. It was written for the man who likes to pursue but didn't think about following through to a relationship. Guarding our hearts is not a justification for walls and fear. It's a rubric to steward the enjoyment of potentially beautiful relationships.

Trust me, the feelings from men to me or me to men have been more than ash-coloured. Should we or shouldn't we date? It's never hard to answer as long as you know how to converse with your heart and with God also.

For a time there was a man I had a huge crush on. Prominent in stature, hot, funny, dark and handsome. He'd text. He'd call. He'd just . . . be there. We'd see each other at socials and he'd invite me to his flat afterwards. One day he told me, 'I always tell my female friends that we are just that – friends.'

But he had never told *me* that. So I'd rest on a silly little hopeful cloud of 'maybe'.

I plucked up the courage once we were both dating other people a year later:

'Can I say something – with no disrespect to our current beaus? You remember that conversation, where you said you always tell a female friend that you see them as just friends? I would have loved you to have had that conversation with me. It left things a little cloudy.'

'Yeah,' he didn't hesitate. 'It was nothing tangible. I couldn't place my finger on it. But with you it was a maybe, yet after a while, I realized a maybe is a no.'

Sometimes hope makes you ignore their maybes. But shield your heart as much as you can against your own lens of seeing the *potential* of a future with someone and instead take what is clear to you in the present.

> **The higher you value yourself, the less you'll settle for his question marks.**

78

The Chase

The higher you value yourself, the less you'll settle for his question marks. If he communicates, if he has clear intention, if you believe he is solid in himself and not hoping for you to fix his world, if he has an intimate relationship with God, placing God at the centre of his world and you outside of it, then you won't have to question the maybe. And, if it is a maybe, be the one to stop the car and hitchhike your way home.

For a real woman never teases the chaser, never needs to toy with him, unless she believes he's worth the follow-through.

Forging hope in a place where there isn't any – whether it is you not saying no to his pursuit, or staying in a friendship where you are secretly wanting more – is a risky game to play. Both come from fear and selfishness.

However the chase looks to you, this is meant to be fun. Enjoy these spontaneous maze-like days and, whatever your personal requests are for being wanted, ensure, above all, that you have provided a safe place within your heart for the Kingdom to reside.

IX

THE RECIPE

'How dare I base love on logical thoughts? This is what it has come to – writing down the desirable virtues of a future man on Café Nero napkins. It is my mind that has complicated the requirements – when Christ made love so simple. Yes. Perhaps it's time to lose the logic and learn to love again.'

(Journal entry, 2013)

'The Recipe' was a concept I devised for a blog post in Her Glass Slipper during 2012. It encouraged your average singleton to list their non-negotiables in order to discover what they were looking for in a healthy relationship – or should I say future spouse. 'What's your recipe?' was a question I regularly asked my friends. One friend took it so seriously, that he arranged a meeting with me, listing twenty-five items, including 'she must look good in sweats'.

The Recipe

'Sweats?' I asked perturbed. 'That's your make or break for marriage? When you are in the middle of confrontation would all be resolved if she changes into a velour Juicy Couture tracksuit?'

'Honestly? Yes.' He told me. 'A girl who can wear sweats is a reflection of so much more.'

I threw the list over my shoulder.

'You are allowed no more than eight things on your list, and they are the non-negotiables. Not a list so tight that the goalposts are standing next to each other. It makes scoring impossible.'

For my list, my requirements were inspired by previous experiences in relationships, all starting with the letter S for memory's sake:

- Secure (both in himself and safe for me)
- Self-sacrificing
- Serious about integrity
- Sexually attractive
- Shapes communities
- Side-splittingly funny (optional bonus)
- Spiritual
- Strong emotional intelligence/maturity

This concept is delightful, perhaps, for dinner games, bus banter, jail time or ensuring an awareness that you're not shopping at 'Boutique Balatron'*. Since igniting this trend in my friends, and having had more than fifty conversations with singles and marrieds, I realize I made a terrible mistake. What I would propound now, is to get a match and burn your lists, for they are as incongruous as a 2-year-old with superglue.

Tables turned when I began to see my single male buddies, who were in their late thirties, still struggling to find their mate. With a wit to match Oscar Wilde and biceps to make Gerard Butler question his manhood, they were all avoiding intimacy because of The Recipe. They'd become too pedantic, too focused on finding their picture perfect woman, missing every exquisite moment placed in front of them, finding the mismatches before they finished their Tiramisu. There was too much reliance on 'other options' available, so there was no patience to sit through date two.

Get a match and burn your lists for they are as incongruous as a 2-year-old with superglue.

They might pray in tongues at 1 p.m. every day, expecting their future wives to be UPSd to their doors at any given Holy Ghost moment, yet when a woman did come along, the list bulldozed the encounter. The Recipe was prioritized over chemistry, over the beautiful essence of interpersonal connection. Any potential relationships were being butchered by fear and exhaustive over-analysis.

You see lists are really tools to comfort the fear of choosing the 'wrong one' for marriage. Lists help you stay emotionless and logical; if this is what love looks like, then Richard Curtis wouldn't have been able to write *Four Weddings and a Funeral* and my movie nights would have been far less satisfactory.

My recipe idea might have been a wise approach in that it helped us think about what to look for in a healthy man. However, when lists become so exhaustive, so precise (unlike mine, ahem) the excuse is, they just really know what they want which, in my translation, means, they are terrified of being in love in case they lose control.

The ingredients for The Recipe came to mind when I had just finished a long-term relationship with a man whom I had hoped one day would be holding my hand in labour while I gave birth to his babies. But through no fault of his, nor perhaps mine, the break-up left my heart a little torn, a little broken, and I became dubious of my own judgement. I created my recipe expecting it would help my discernment, or, more honestly, bring back hope.

If you are dating a guy who has this list lasered on his brain, might I suggest you will find more enjoyment at the helm of fourteenth-century torture methods in the Tower of London. You think I'm joking?

Of course my statistical analysis is way off par to suggest this will always be the case, but, in my humble experience, men and women who own extreme expectations are often successful, independent, charming, popular, able to run off an Emerson quote for every life problem, with at least three party tricks up their sleeve. Their intimacy with the Lord may be questionable but, of course, if this isn't on your list, then you can shove that under the carpet until it bites you on the derrière.

I have dated a couple of these guys (at different times you understand), ones who wanted their woman to be free, have a mind that could rule a government, be chirpy, love God, weigh 15 lb less than their current weight, have original thought, be fun, confident, sexy, challenging, soft, confrontational to the point of him being seen for who he is, but not so confrontational that he questions himself. All of this, while reciting from Proverbs 31 'Charm is deceptive, and beauty is fleeting; but a woman who fears the LORD is to be praised'.

One hated my vintage wardrobe so much, I found myself wearing dull attire to dodge the criticism; it was like dating Captain Von Trap without a convent to escape to.

Ladies, if a man is *adding* to the Proverbs 31 wife requirements, you're playing Sonic the Hedgehog without a control pad and it's game over before you've had a chance to ever be known.

It's dire living your everyday with a man who will analyse you, conferring with his support network on concerns that arise rather than conferring with you. One hated my vintage wardrobe so much, I found myself wearing dull attire to dodge the criticism; it was like dating Captain Von Trap without a convent to escape to. The list, the logical analysis, the 'I must hear from the Lord' tag line, became an excuse to disrespect a woman, to not cover her heart, but helpfully opened up one major lesson to me:

You don't need a list – not if you can trust yourself and have been conversing with God for a long time about what he wants for you. You are more open-minded to accepting and loving people as they are, if you love you.

I'm no mad-dash fan of writing love letters to the future spouse, or dreaming all the time about the 'better half'. I fear it creates a co-dependency or fantasy-like stance on a person that will be flawed. It will also distract us from working on ourselves, when we should be looking at being healthier, being a good teammate and thinking about – this is important – what we can give them, not what they can give us.

When we love who we are, the list needn't be written down in so much accuracy nor tattooed on the thigh. Talk to the Lord about what's right for you in marriage before that person ever enters your life.

'Carrie, I think you should begin to write down in a new journal what you desire in a husband,' my pastor shared.

'Bit cheesy, isn't it?' I responded, hesitant to waste a precious Moleskine* on such sentiments.

'My wife gave me her journal on our wedding night. She had been writing in it before she ever met me.'

Now this was a guy whose marriage I really admired. Accountable to the very diaper he's changing, he adored his wife and she adored him. They were healthy, happy, interdependent and wise within a very expressive and liberated love.

So I was willing to listen.

'Oh but my list has proven to be more of a hindrance,' I replied.

In our conversation I realized I hadn't really created The Recipe in conversation with God, but out of fear of all the surrounding relationships I'd ever witnessed to be bad. And by now you'll know that anything cooked from fear is a coronary waiting to happen.

So I began to write in conversation with God what I desired for my future husband – for us, not for myself. I prayed for his family, his heart, his wants. I didn't specify regarding appearance (I've dated enough beautiful men to know this is about longevity – not arm candy), or even characteristics, because a man who truly loves the Lord will bring the fruits of the Spirit anyway. A kindness that feeds not his own desires but his desires for family and love. A faithfulness that rests in the inheritance of his salvation, rather than hiding behind his family or job. A self-control that focuses on one woman at

In that moment, a continual conversation proved more powerful than the eight bullet points etched into my conscience. I became less of a perfectionist more of a lover.

a time, not a wandering eye waiting for the upgrade that will only disappoint. A goodness that allows humility to always promote growth. A peace that silences the storms. A patience that wins victories and a love that can't help but beckon questions from strangers.

'Once you've had clearer conversations with the Lord on this whole area, the man for you to date is highlighted the moment they walk in the room,' so my pastor told me. In that moment, a continual conversation proved more powerful than the eight bullet points etched into my conscience. I became less of a perfectionist, more of a lover, spotting other list-carriers a mile off.

In reaction to a new perspective, I soon attracted a very different type of man. Perhaps they were there all along and my eyes were completely hidden to them. But whether it was the businessman in an airport tracking me down when I had no make-up on and giving me his card, or a lawyer at the top of the Gansevoort Hotel sharing his heart about the book of Job (an unexpected topic in a venue like that), the heart-calibre of man was changing. I was finding the ones who cared what they could give to the world, not for what the world could give to them.

When you invite the Author of Salvation to be the author of your romance, the experiences surpass your humble beginnings and together you write the greatest of stories to be told for the hope of the generations to come.

X

CREEPY CRAWLIES

'O sons, listen to me, and do not depart from the words of my mouth. Keep your way far from her, and do not go near the door of her house, lest you give your honour to others and your years to the merciless.'

(Proverbs 5:7–9, ESV)

Creepy Crawlies are the hybrid of modern Christian dating. They are the counter-culture to the counter-cultural view of Christianity. They do have phobias, but not of commitment, like so much of the jury will assume. No. Their phobia lies in the fear of intimacy or, more precisely, being intimate with the *wrong one*. They might have graduated with a degree in 'Obtaining the Ladies', but keeping a girl? That's a shuddersome thought.

Please understand, I know there are as many women who tease as there are these men who chase, but as I'm seeing this trend increase inside the church (a trend staying put for the moment), this is an important subject to broach. Because for as long as this fear is allowed to kill off fish with its oil-slick-like infestation, people will never unite in the only thing that can still shock the world – love.

For the Creepy Crawlies (CCs), the chase is over once they've achieved the catch. The fish are chucked right back into the water. You are the fish. OK I am. I am the fish. We are all the

They might have graduated with a degree in 'Obtaining the Ladies', but keeping a girl? That's a shuddersome thought.

fish at the end of the Creepy Crawlies' mission.

Let me tell you about the Creepy Crawlies because boy have I met a few and, so far, they are losing in the fishing stakes, as unbelievers just lead by their gut with a pinch of politeness, snatching all the ladies away. And I sometimes don't blame the women for going. I'm not suggesting we get out of town and run away with any man who sweeps us off our feet. There are enough Christian boys who do the sweeping; it's their maintenance that I'm suggesting we need to look at.

Creepy Crawlies' 'happy place' is somewhere between their leather-bound journal and their latest man crush. Proverbs 31 is etched into their amygdala, if not tattooed on their butt. They are emotionless, and keep it so to excuse the 134 hours they've spent with you in their 168-hour week. They need to be the centre of attention. They hate to be placed on a pedestal but equally hate to be challenged, especially if you've been hurt by a genuine mistake they made; because they are perfectionists. They need to have a material seal of approval delivered from Christ himself to say you are a *potential* prospect. Their spirit of comparison is volatile as they compare you with their ex-girlfriend, their mum, their pit bull, their car, the girlfriends dating all of the males they share bromance with, the bromance itself, the other profiles they've been checking out online ('But I have a pure heart!' they each cry), and their past victims who've not made the cut.

Whatever they do, they will not let go until you allow them to be your hero – if just for one day. As my friend Markus Kirwald explains: 'Men like to be in control. They like to hunt for something, and once they have it they strive for something else. Just looking at a lot of those relationships out there is scary. The men I look up to are rare. Either guys don't know how to treat women or they don't care. Show me your friends and I'll tell you who you are. Looking at the wrong people as their idol and trying to be a carbon copy of somebody else becomes the standard. Guys don't know how to love right and there are not enough leaders out there who lead the men into a healthy relationship.'[10]

Sadly we can't compare dating dilemmas to those Christ had, because he kept his eyes on the glory prize; but some days, just some days, I wish he had led an example of a week of veracious dating. Can you imagine if he had? We'd all have that special story to reference in any dating dilemmas.

Christ was a son, he was a lover and he was a servant. The only three vitals you need look for in a steadfast man.

How a man treats everyone around him is indicative to how he sees himself. So if a man is fishing with nets instead of fishing with one hook, the lack of exclusivity is indicative of his own self-image.

If a man is fishing with nets instead of fishing with one hook, the lack of exclusivity is indicative of his own self-image.

When Christ told Simon Peter et al. to toss their nets to the right side of the boat in order to catch more fish, Simon Peter celebrated at the catch and enjoyed their much-anticipated breakfast. However, in today's society, and in my version of today's story, it goes something like this:

Simon Peter: 'Bring in the fish? No, Jesus! I couldn't possibly *keep* them. How else am I supposed to validate my own self-esteem if I just *eat* them? What do you think this is? Hanukkah? I'm going to decline your offer and keep spending my days rowing around the lake, placing the nets where I can catch different fish and throw them back into the lake, to do it all over again tomorrow. Maybe I'll find the crème de la crème of halibut finally and then I will be victorious!'

Jesus: 'Excellent idea. Why don't you chuck some hydrochloric acid in there at the same time and really revel in your self-loathing?'

Simon Peter: 'What?'

Some Creepy Crawlies run around comparing multiple women in the hope they make the right choice but, even once they have committed to a relationship, they still wrestle in their mind with thoughts such as: 'Oh God, what if I have made the wrong decision? My life is over and I'm trapped with this woman, who could become my WIFE.' Vulnerability is not an option. They find a flaw, and off they pop, to their next hunt. What they fail to notice is that they are the victim of their own torturous, over-analytical, no time to find true love, nightmare.

What's worse is that post-modern women have become so scared of this untrustworthy character that we each become our own protector – not believing that anyone, not even our Father, will fight for us, hedging our bets to see who's worth the risk of allowing into our world. We become overly protective. We've lost hope of ever finding men who have the testicular fortitude to follow through, not just to a relationship but to actually allow themselves to become vulnerable, to become intimate, to show us their flaws and know they can still be loved, while still being challenged.

Aggressive feminists may have become a little too gung-ho with their approach. I was all for the suffragettes, but when we attempt to replace a man's fight, it's all gone terribly wrong. Men weren't made to be berated by a woman's tongue. Neither were women created to be the experiment for a man's love laboratory.

We've got to change the game plan, friends. Look out for these guys, and be discerning, for your time is as precious as the appearance of the Northern Lights.

Dating a CC is disheartening. I've spent one too many months being patient, staying attached to a relationship just in case he *is* Mr Potential but each week becoming more and more alarmed by his self-sabotaging behaviour.

But some people do learn.

Because, when I was 18, I was the female version of a Creepy Crawly. Yes. You didn't see that coming, did you?

I had 'contacts' everywhere. From work. My gym. The youth work. The theatre company I was part of. The Quaker meeting (I don't mean the brand of porridge). The yoga class. The parties I couldn't get enough of. Little effort was exerted for that second glance to reel them in; the sentence that would make him feel empowered by me; a joke to get him enjoying my company. A skip and a wink and I was outta there. The same thing to different men. They all had my number. I had theirs. Many a night was had with enjoyable banter and exchanges of sweet digital sentiment. But none of it went anywhere, because getting close would mean risk. As I sized each one up, checking out their body measurements, wisdom, sense of humour, level of advanced flirtatiousness, dancing ability, how much they *really* loved God, ambition, diction, poise, comfortable in their surroundings, philosophical debate, eyes, athleticism and whether they could outwit me. The comparisons just went on and on. Until no one was good enough and I became bored – lazy as sin.

The comparisons just went on and on. Until no one was good enough and I became bored.

I knew it got too much when I was 20. Three different men came in unannounced to the shop where I worked, all wanting to see me during my lunch break. As I hid behind the counter of the main sales desk, I whispered to a colleague, 'Something's gotta give.' In a second I heard the Lord say: *Yes. You.*

I had hurt his sons. Any emotional attention given to more than one man at a time, even in my heart – I knew the Lord could see it. He knew it wasn't pure. I walked down the hall to my locker, bowed my head and said, 'I'm sorry'. I watched them, all three of them, on surveillance camera, waiting for me to come from the back. All expectant. None of them knowing of each other's existence in the shop. One of them I'd known for a while and, as I watched him almost excited to know he was surprising me, tears rolled down my face. I couldn't go out. I was too ashamed.

Never again after that did I trump-card or mess about emotionally with multiple men. Although I hadn't kissed any of them, it didn't matter. I had played with their thoughts and that's enough to make my soul misshapen, never mind theirs.

Not investing fully into one woman or one man exclusively is down to fear. People without identity mask themselves, so they fall into performance. As Shakespeare wrote: 'God has given you one face, and you make yourself another.'[11] If only they would drop the pack of cards instead of trying to play them right.

Creepy Crawlies need spiritual fathers who emit an air of respect when they walk into a room, owning their own unshakable identity. Under their guidance CCs can grow, and see for themselves that true love can be found among their mess.

Ladies, this isn't about you. It really isn't. Although if you're waiting around for the man with a fear of intimacy (philophobe) to make some revelatory discovery that you're perfect for him, then I might suggest you have the same illness and should consult a doctor – better yet, a friend who will be honest with you.

The pursuit is enjoyable, but it's only the first hurdle. Most adults who have really experienced the ecstasy of true love will tell you that. The art is the maintenance of keeping it, treasuring it as much as if it were the first day you set eyes on each other. Over the years your love grows even more. But within the chase much performance is used to catch you. When you begin to date, the bravado can't be held up for long. You become a cellophane bag filled with water like the ones hanging over Borough Market's fish stall. The bags create a reflection for flies – which makes them dart away. It's the same with intimacy. People need to learn to face their own reflection from another point of view. It is how they handle self-actualization.

Some CCs will find younger girls that think they hung the moon. Other men will relish the challenge, but will go through painstaking trials to hopefully learn that the key to finding 'the one' is in the acceptance of themself.

When true love strikes, it's dynamite. But you won't encounter it with creeps who crawl around looking for spare change.

For me, well I decided to find some guts and, as my value grew in learning God's wild acceptance of me, just as I am, I was willing to allow someone to see all my flaws by the time I was 27. To this day, that five-year boyfriend still cares very much for me and for all who are in my life. When I've gone through break-ups, he's been the first to tell me how brilliant I am, and he's the last person I'd have thought would say such things.

After witnessing so much fear in dating, so much fear once men were dating women, the light bulb flicked on during an afternoon lecture I attended: 'Intimacy is painful, but the benefits of covenant far outweigh the pain of covenant. If you're going to commit to someone you're going to have pain. This isn't about the world being comfortable; it's not meant to be comfortable.'[12]

When true love strikes, it's dynamite. But you won't encounter it with creeps who crawl around looking for spare change. Wait in a singular fashion; stand solid as a girl who refuses to settle.

The Creepy Crawly rarely ends up with the bride of unreachable dreams, but the Lord will endeavour to show them, moment-by-moment, girl-by-girl, that the only way to true love is through a servant heart, through a teachable heart.

The prideless heart is as perennial as the grass and as fragrant as a lavender field. I can't wait for the day when people, no matter their gender, will discover the truth in a moment of awakening. For that will be the day when they truly learn to love.

CARRIE'S PRACTICAL POINTERS

- Boys are great. But so are YOU. You want to be chosen, sought after, desired. It's in our make up to scream out, 'Chase me! Chase me!' So learn to take your time, so you can gauge how they are in friendship settings, difficult circumstances, honesty, family, dreams. **Enjoy being a friend to them first. There is no rush.**

- Are they scouring the room for other options of women, or are their eyes only on you? That tribal mentality, the searching around, is an indication that a guy doesn't really know who he is, therefore doesn't know what he wants. **You don't want a guy who is fishing with a net, instead of a hook.**

- Give men a chance. Scratching them off the list because of 'chubby ankles' is not appreciating men of depth. **If you're not feeling it after date one or even just some hang-outs, be honest and (gently) explain why.** You will help the guy immensely.

- Set your standard as being utterly truthful from the beginning – be it online, at a coffee, in social gatherings. **Be real. Communicate.** Then clarify where you stand:

whether he's mentioned something or not. This protects your heart from false hope, and communicates to him that you value the friendship over anything else.

- Get spiritual brothers and fathers. 'Brothers' are men whom you've honestly communicated with – you've both declared you have no interest in each other but value friendship. **Such men will cover you, giving you helpful male advice** and will also challenge you on those 'blind spots' where they feel you are not helping yourself.

- **There are no maybes.** Hanging out in one-to-one settings with men without telling them how you feel (or don't feel) about them, even if you haven't been physical, is still teasing. If I've made friends with a man I usually define our friendship within a few weeks.

- **Lists are useless** if they are not developed in conversation with God. Your designer knows you better than you do. So ask him what's a suitable partner for you, then **begin with a servant-like attitude: how can you serve each other?** What can you put into the relationship?

- **Playing the 'God' card when declining a date shirks responsibility.** Be gracious and turn them down politely, but always take ownership of your own opinions. Involve God in prayer as you go through any process of the pursuit; this is what makes you powerful as a woman of God.

PART III

LOOKING BEFORE YOU LEAP

You're dating. (Yay!) But do you marry? (Ahhh.) The 'love drug' can create a few miscalculations in many relationships. We get a little ahead of the game, planning table settings and honeymoons before the first month of courtship is even over. Perhaps he's the best of the bunch on offer, or you're settling for one too many mismatches. Co-dependents beware, as this section challenges the neediest of women, poking the softest of spots. But challenge we must, as I believe that dating the same person for a space of time will help you decide if you're marrying for the right reasons (super), or for 'fixing' reasons (no no). How long do you fight to keep him, and when should you let him go? As we grow in the ever more complex world, the key is to keep our relationships simple, filled with honour and – oh yes – joy.

XI

'YOU'LL DO'

> 'No one's ever seen or heard anything like this;
> Never so much as imagined anything quite like it –
> What God has arranged for those who love him.'
>
> (1 Corinthians 2:9, *The Message*)

'Have you popped your cherry yet, Carrie?'

This question was a sweet sentiment messaged to me from a friend I'd not heard from since 1998. This same girlfriend had invented this monotonous question back then for everyone in my class to ask me in corridors, during lunch breaks and on blackboards; using any method that could make this a public announcement. I was the last virgin of my year and I had planned to keep it that way until marriage. While the news broadcast Bill Clinton denying having sexual relations with Monica Lewinsky, I, apparently, wasn't having enough.

I responded to the weighted question:

'Alas, I "popped" it a while back.'

'Are you married?' she asked instantly.

'No.'

'I'm disappointed,' she replied.

'Why? You made my life hell for not doing so?'

'Honestly? I would trade places with you to avoid *that* conversation with a man I like about how many people I've slept with. But you, we had faith in you; you were the benchmark. Instead – you settled.'

She was right. I had settled for the here and now, for the 'it's never going to happen because no man will wait for me'.

When we're told as children of God that we should aim for excellence and aim high, why do we settle for mediocre? Why do we settle for the deep-fried cheese when we could consider the 12 oz lobster?

Why do we settle for the deep-fried cheese when we could consider the 12 oz lobster?

It could be the secretarial job you stayed in for a decade when you wanted to be headteacher. It could be the relationship with the man who treats your heart like a workbench. It could be that you're aging and you feel you have to lessen your goals or core values for marriage, fearful your ovaries will run off into the sunset without you.

104

'You'll Do'

You can bet your Book of Common Prayer that the older you get the more you believe your biological clock is coming to get you, hunt you down, pin you to the ground and shout into your ear that you are now past it at the age of 26 (especially in Christian time zones). It's time to seek therapy, become a middle-aged cattery owner or chuck yourself off a cliff.

But there is another option. 'If you haven't found it yet, keep looking. Don't settle. As with all matters of the heart, you'll know when you find it. And, like any great relationship, it just gets better and better as the years roll on.'[13]

Fear, comfort, distrust, lethargy and hopelessness are all part and parcel of the problem. We live in a disposable society where buildings are thrown up quickly and fall down in a week, where Wal-Mart and Primark are doing better than Harrods because businessmen have seen how we're settling for cheap over quality and longevity.

The sixty-second viral has pushed aside Warhol's fifteen minutes of fame. No one would watch a fifteen-minute viral. Few have the patience or fight to get to the end – just like marriage.

So, unless I'm guaranteed that Jared Leto will be my husband (once he falls in love with Christ), I'm expected to settle for the guy sitting next to me on the Tube whose name I'm yet to know but who will be the father of my future ticking-time-bomb kids.

Where's your worth? Does it crave instant gratification, or could your value allow you the patience to elevate you to the excellence you were destined for?

You? I believe you're the Aretha Franklin of the new age, screeching for R.E.S.P.E.C.T. You're the Oprah Winfrey who got fired for being a 'terrible reporter' in her first job then went on to become the first billionaire African-American woman. You're the Thomas Edison who finally, on his thousandth attempt, invented the first practical incandescent light bulb.

You're the girl who was held at gunpoint by North Korean Communists with many other Christians in a local church hall. Their choice was to either deny the existence of Christ by spitting on a picture of Jesus as they walked out alive, or be shot in the head. You're the girl in this story who, after watching men and women older than her spit on the picture of Christ, hoping to save their lives, walked up to the picture, wiped it down with her skirt and went back to the middle of the room. She, at 11 years of age, uttered the words, 'I am willing to die'. She was ready to be shot because she refused to settle. The tribal gunman backed down, baffled by her courage.[14]

You're her. You're the fighter. You're an outrageous dreamer who, no matter what your circumstances, no matter how tragic your past, no matter how many times you've screwed up, fights for who you believe in – and that's the author of time.

As Mandela said: 'You are a child of God. Your playing small does not serve the world. There is nothing enlightened about your shrinking so that people won't feel insecure around you. We are born to make manifest the glory of God that is within us. It's not just in some of us; it's in all of us and, as we are liberated from our own fear, our presence automatically liberates others.'[15]

You heard Mandela – it's in all of us.

And what about what God says? 'You were not a mistake, for all your days are written in my book.'[16]

God gave up everything he had in the hope that he would gain your love. That love not only looks like conversation, it looks like action. It looks like blood, sweat and tears. It looks like saying no to unhealthy men and seeking to listen to your heart first. It stretches outside the comfort zones quicker than *Big Brother*. It looks like seeking him with all of your heart in your day job, in your relationships and in your silence.

The less you settle, the easier relationships become. Trust me, darling.

If you desire a man who covers you, who thinks about your heart, who is honest, who isn't afraid to lead, a man you fancy as much as Chris Pine* – then let it be so, because you're allowed to have standards. In fact, it's imperative that you do if you're seeking men who also have standards.

You don't just hop on to the next bus that comes along, you check the destination first, don't you? So why don't you consider the destination before getting all hoity-toity with boys? Because of emotional needs? Something you need to get fixed there? Go to your emotional mechanics (God, mentors, friends), not a man who bruises your heart a little with something different every week.

Once you raise the bar, great men do soon come into view.

The less you settle, the easier relationships become. Trust me, darling.

To settle would reinforce a lack of trust in a provider, in a heaven that seeks purposefully to bring you the man you desire (ensuring we can steward healthy men and relationships well). To settle would slip a note to your inner-self, 'You are a big dreamer – they don't actually exist'.

As one who has settled in the past, I'm now determined to give up on mediocre for good. Should you hear of accusations of high maintenance, they've not seen the marriages I have, that knew what to fight for and what not to fight for.

In the aim of avoiding settling, but not colluding with perfectionism, I began to ask three simple questions to ensure I gave a healthy start to a potentially long-term relationship:

- Are they teachable? Or does pride consistently get in the way?

- Are they Kingdom cuckoo? Let's hope so.
- Do they love the Lord and show that in their love for you?

You need to get fed up of mediocre; don't stand for it any more. Once you raise the bar, great men do soon come into view. Living your life like it's platinum takes a lot of focus, dedication and a willingness to not go back to living in reaction to past experiences. Making the decision that platinum treatment is what you were designed for ensures you will keep the pewter lifestyle at bay.

XII

PACE, DARLING

'Rest in the LORD, and wait patiently for him.'
(Psalm 37:7, KJV)

If only people came with a health-warning label, then we might be prepared for that instantaneous love-at-a-second glance encounter. It's takes one moment for someone to enter your life – their name etched in your memory, no matter how much you may later attempt to eradicate it.

Patience in pace is where true love forms and where mistakes – relationships aptly known as 'hideous' – are easily avoided. I have made the misjudgement of thinking I've met the one I should marry, only to find myself, months later, pushing the business card of a reputable therapist under their doormat and changing my mobile number. Twice I've introduced my friends to the new boyfriend saying, 'I think this is it.' OK, maybe three times. However, I've desisted rushing in with such finite statements after a faux pas that made me so nauseous I developed an addiction to Pepto-Bismol. There is nothing worse than looking back on a relationship that you realize was fast-paced for very unhealthy reasons.

Not too long ago, I was listening to a lecture by a life coach discussing 'the marriage ladder'. Healthy steps to check as you move up towards marriage. 'I've got this in the bag,' I thought to myself, smiling like a Cheshire cat with double cream. I was in a relationship with a man who, despite a previous unhealthy relationship, seemed pretty healed from the split. He could recite every quote about grace, led worship at his local church, had a nice sense of humour, was sociable, dedicated to his local community and we both liked Gruyère. So, of course, I could see no cause for alarm and got on the love toboggan with no wish to hinder the momentum. Within a week of dating, he mentioned he thought about marriage.

Here was my problem. I didn't stop that thought process, in fact I even engaged in such conversations for some weeks. Could he be the answer to my lifelong search? The love that inspired Tennessee Williams? Was I the bow to his arrow?

We entered into a long-distance relationship only eleven weeks later. Knowing it would be challenging for the relationship, I even offered to part ways for his sake as I was moving to California for nine months. He had no intention of finishing it, and was kindly willing to fight. We managed for about four weeks until the cracks began to make excruciating noises. I was growing faster than ever before with my new adventure the other side of the world. I soon learnt that your own growth can intimidate the partner watching unless they're secure in themselves. He became fearful of losing me altogether. Criticism of my change began to arise. Controlling behaviours and disconnection in conversation became more apparent and yet mentions of marriage kept popping up.

I soon asked him to stop using the M word. I wanted to feel known as a woman in her own right, not a girl holding someone's happy ending. I wanted us to learn more about each other before making a life decision.

Let's cut back to the marriage ladder talk . . . My buttons got triggered when I heard: 'If they're pushing the pace quicker than you wish it to go, they're trying to fix something within.'

I sat in my seat for ten minutes after everyone else had left the class, staring at the now completed marriage ladder on the whiteboard. I'm not easily swayed by others' opinions, but I couldn't deny this was why I was feeling lonely in the relationship. I flew back for Christmas and, when I opened a present from him, found a leather-bound 'to do list' book that included pages detailing possible honeymoon destinations. It had gone too far. That night I cried all the way home, stopping off for a McChicken Sandwich (I never eat McDonald's) after feeling like I was just a sock to mute the noise of his own pain. I wasn't heard, I wasn't understood and, with one more mention of me being his 'future wife', I found no option but to end the relationship. He believed he meant well, but I was being used as an emotional Band-Aid as my cries, my needs, my heart, were being ignored.

Either they slow it down or, like a husky owner, refuse to see just how much dog hair they carry on their own jumper.

There are only so many times you can confront something like this. Either they slow it down or, like a husky owner, refuse to see just how much dog hair they carry on their own jumper.

Billy Graham's wife once said she would have married the wrong man four times if God had given her the person that she had thought was right for her at the time. She eventually found the right person because she wanted God's best, and he kept her from making the wrong choice.

Pace is the antithesis of panic. People intoxicated by love shout, 'Why wait!?' to which I now respond, 'Why rush?!' Marriage cannot be dictated by your infatuated emotions, by your burning loins, by your need to have children, by your wish to end loneliness, by your need to be loved, by your desire to register for a Saks Fifth Avenue wedding list, by your need to have sex (again), by your need to hide behind the glow of someone's adoration, by a hope that your future will be saved by someone else's fortune, by the need to be completed, by the need for your life to start or in order to rewrite the ending to a previous heinous relationship.

As Van Epp explains, 'If attachment is the glue in relationships, then an accelerated attachment is like superglue. It activates a willingness to overlook and minimize obvious problems.'[17]

The reason why I wrote this book in the first place was not to give advice on how to find Prince Sebastian in all his royal military regalia. It was actually to encourage each one of us to learn to be whole in ourselves, to learn the joy of self-love – something that has become lost amongst many of my contemporaries. It is something I've only discovered for myself in recent years.

> **I don't believe in 'the one'. I believe in a premier league of 'ones' from a celestial supply; it's only at engagement that we make them 'the one'.**

So let me state once and for all: I don't believe in 'the one'. I believe in a premier league of 'ones' from a celestial supply; it's only at engagement that we make them 'the one'. Had I stuck to the theory that there is only 'the one' for each of us, I would have jeopardized the entire cosmos, missing 'the one' by veering off the yellow brick road, going to Starbucks instead of Jamba Juice one morning. Had I believed that every man I dated might be 'the one', I'd have had a nervous breakdown every time I went through a break-up. Precipitance only occurs when we're pressing the panic button in a drought of options.

'The one' is not to be rushed, they are to be researched, reached into – spiritually speaking.

Life is simpler when your love for the Lord is stronger than the desire for the man flexing his biceps in front of you. Like Ruth Graham, knowing what he desires the most really has made it feasible for much healthier marriages to take place. As my friend Abi Classey told me:

'I'm discovering only now. two years after a divorce. that the intimacy I so craved, the connection I so desired from being married and having sex was actually a pointer to the intimacy I desperately needed from God. Ultimately, I wanted to be known and accepted, loved, cherished and desired by a

Please hear me: pleasant pace is not to be confused with fear. Pleasant pace trusts in God's timing; fear has no recollection of God at all.

man. But the craving in my heart was beyond those things. It was really a search for identity, self-worth and feeling valued for who I was as a woman.'[18]

When it comes to people who rush towards marriage, I often advise they purposely push back the pace to test if the relationship is able to survive. In my personal example, when I did just that, control and manipulation came from someone who 'loved' me. The test is whether they honour you or they slam your name. Any fast-paced panic is due to them needing to fix a need in themselves . . .

There can be too much caution in the Christian dater: fear of making the wrong decision or committing to the wrong one. Not following through is as common as the custard creams served on Sunday. Please hear me: pleasant pace is not to be confused with fear. Pleasant pace trusts in God's timing; fear has no acknowledgement of God at all.

Enjoy the tension of being in love and relish the dating. Enjoy the moment rather than dreaming of veils and satin Diors. The commitment you need is to be found in the man you'll sacrifice your days for over and over. The pace is a nod to the man who's willing to lay down his life just as Christ died for the church.

There are, however, some cases, my parents included, who buck such trends. My father, who had dated a string of sixties models 'with nothing between the ears', was in a season of wishing to find one of character, of substance, of intellect. To be honest, he wasn't really looking; he was quite content in his own life. Often, that's the key that shows God you're ready to steward the real thing.

My mother was cute, but not knockout enough to cause a beeline in a canteen. Not until my father spotted her, of course. He was mid-conversation, discussing F.F. Bruce or Tolstoy no doubt with his boys, when he looked up across his dinner tray and said, 'I'm sorry to interrupt lads, but I think I'm going to marry that girl over there.'

'What?'

'I'm sorry . . . Continue.'

His conversation with the Lord just as mentioned in 'The Recipe' chapter, was the reason I acknowledge that there are exceptions to the rule. That afternoon, the professor of the college introduced my father and mother, and he asked my father to show her around the college for her research paper.

As he often shared over the dinner table, putting me off my poached salmon for the rest of the evening:

'Let's just say, Carrie, I never did show your mother the rest of the college. If you know what I mean.'

'OH DAD! DUDE!'

'I held her hand.'

'Oh . . . right . . . well.'

'And we were unofficially engaged twenty-four hours later. Married in six months.'

My parents were happily married for thirty-six years. Their love was very real, very beautiful and not to be sniffed at. Dedicated from the moment they met, sacrificing themselves to each other, they created a great team of woven love and light. They saved many marriages from the brink, and rescued many more people from choosing inappropriate people to marry.

That consistent conversation in the depths of the soul, before a significant other even enters the room for the first time, in the humility of asking ourselves honest questions against the desires of infatuation, is the vital component to making sure the engine of a relationship is running on healthy, functioning cylinders.

Never must pace be dictated by just our thoughts and feelings, but it must be interwoven in the very tapestry of God's wisdom, for his desires go beyond what you think you are capable of. So let me ask: do you believe the man for you will exceed your greatest expectations?

XIII

NOT TONIGHT ROMEO

'You're blessed when you meet Lady Wisdom,
when you make friends with Madame Insight.
She's worth far more than money in the bank;
her friendship is better than a big salary.
Her value exceeds all trappings of wealth;
nothing you could wish for holds a candle to her.
With one hand she gives long life,
with the other she confers recognition.
Her manner is beautiful,
her life is wonderfully complete.
She's the very Tree of Life to those who embrace her.'
(Proverbs 3:13–18, *The Message*)

Dare I suggest that during the suicide scene of *Romeo and Juliet*, Lady Wisdom had left the building? Perhaps if she were present, Romeo would have checked Juliet's pulse before knocking back deadly poison?

Might I also propose that these two characters were the greatest co-dependents of the Shakespearean era and yet we've learnt nothing from this fable. In fact a recent report proposed that 40 million (mostly) women in the United States of America are labelled co-dependent.[19] That's a whole lotta crazy sister; a crazy that I dream will change so that we can learn to really love judiciously.

I want to see women stand strong within their own boundaries; be unoffendable because they know their identity; no longer control or manipulate but trust men; allow men to make mistakes; no longer avoid feelings as if they are a curse but give their hearts a voice; enjoy intimacy instead of being terrified of it; break free from the role of being caretakers of other people's problems but instead have compassion without judgemental fixing.

Unlike Romeo and Juliet, I don't want to die because the one I love had a power nap.

Ladies, your man is just that: a man. He is not the macaroni to your cheese, the bubbles to your bath, the milk to your cookie, nor the smile to your face. It's all pretty poetry but the reality is that co-dependency creates malfunctioning relationships, cripples futures and brings destruction along its path. It steals, kills and destroys – remind you of anyone?

Co-dependency is an international plague that's seeping into our day and the creator of this illness is the very enemy to love. Thank you *Love Actually*, but *Fatal Attraction** probably had a more realistic message.

Unlike Romeo and Juliet, I don't want to die because the one I love had a power nap. That is, allow other people's behaviours to dictate my own worth. Co-dependency is infatuation, addiction, irrationality and insecurity; it's basically anything *but* love. Love feeds growth, while co-dependency kicks it in the shins. As Plato said: 'People are like dirt. They can either nourish you and help you grow as a person or they can stunt your growth and make you wilt and die.'[20]

When God told us to love he didn't mean we should stalk people on our computer screens, call them every waking minute of the day or resent them for their own journey in life. True love means not drowning your sorrows with absinthe, not destroying a good night's sleep by worrying over what *they* think of you, nor having two fingers for dessert*

Yes, people can become obsessed by the need to cure another person's problem. You react in ways that become so distracting that you've lost track of your own purpose in life.

because you think society won't accept you if you can't wear jeggings.

121

You can't love your neighbour if you allow fear to make you hate yourself. This isn't just about relationships. This is about anything that you're using to fix low self-esteem or a broken past. You name it, you could make it your obsession: Absolut vodka, MDMA, sex, social media, money, an addictive relative (yes, people can become obsessed by the need to cure another person's problem). You react in ways that become so distracting that you've lost track of your own purpose in life.

As Melody Beattie says, 'Co-dependents are reactionaries. They overreact. They under-react. But rarely do they act. They react to the problems, pains, lives, and behaviours of others. They react to their own problems, pains, and behaviours.'[21]

For me, co-dependency manifested in a number of ways. Firstly, in addiction. At 21, when my university mates were getting wasted on WKD, I was in what Hollywood filmmakers would call 'the rooms'. The home to AA, OA, NA, GA and, oh I don't know, 'I'm addicted to squashed-faced cats anonymous'.

Around this time an eating disorder occurred, not because I saw pictures of triple-zero women at the Emmy Awards, but because I couldn't control circumstances in my life. Instead of communicating my hurt, or accepting that my dad and/or boyfriend's alcohol addiction was not a sign that they didn't love me, the only logical solution for me at the time was to sweat on a treadmill, not eat and monitor my hipbones in photographs.

There were a couple of celebrities at that time who I observed closely, via glossy prints and emulated in the skeletal look (once you find a reason for sabotage you'll use media to back it up). Irony struck when I sat next to a pop star in the 'rooms'. The same A-lister celebrity I had been getting 'healthy' food tips from in women's fashion monthlies. She was in this disorder as much as I was.

I repudiated anorexia when I lost social friends (I was always in the gym) and, well, I got hungry – for bacon. The root of co-dependency was still there though. Years later I fell in love with a man who rocked my world so much that I lost myself in the earthquake. Had I met him today, I'd have seen how different we were in seconds. But I wanted to rewrite my past issue with the death of my father by fixing the boyfriend, instead of myself.

I wanted marriage before a sexual relationship, yet I settled for sex after a short time of dating. This was the same girl who hadn't had sex with her previous boyfriend because we were 'Christians'. I believed in nothing hidden, he liked his privacy. I didn't want to co-habit before marriage, he already had. I compromised myself so I could keep him in my life. When your mind and spirit are screaming at you internally, your body begins to malfunction. I lost myself, which, in turn, made me have to lose him.

The level of intimacy exceeded the level of trust. Shame ate away as I knew I was compromising my own values. Finally, he wasn't allowed to be imperfect because imperfection meant

I was at risk of being hurt by him falling off the pedestal I'd placed him on. My perfectionism caused him to lie and his lies destroyed my trust. This vicious web we wove was destructive despite the fact that he really was a wonderful man and I was a girl he utterly loved. It was a relationship that could have survived without the insecurity that maimed us, but we didn't know how to love ourselves for the sake of each other.

It was during this relationship that my co-dependency ended. I didn't want it to affect my mind, my body and therefore my spirit any more. I was broken and finally realized that manipulation is as beneficial as espresso before you sleep. I loved him too much to allow this vicious circle to continue.

To be alive again, taking ownership was cardinal. I took my fingers out of my ears and reached out to friends who could keep me focused on healing, not self-condemnation. It took forgiveness, listening to God above any other human voice, being accountable to those I trusted all the while ridding myself of guilt and any other lie that said I didn't deserve radical love.

You don't want to end up being *that* girl, like my friend's friend. The girl who tied herself to the washing line in the back garden after a huge disagreement with her boyfriend. She had been asked to leave, but instead decided to hold onto his leg while he dragged his left femur down the corridor. It took the police to remove her from the washing line.

The police.

Eating disorders and pinning yourself to clothes lines aside, it only takes a whiff of expectation just that centimetre too high for a healthy, confident person to run an extra mile while an unhealthy person stays not static but inwardly dying. There is no such thing as plateau.

Do you want to be that needy girl who becomes the burden in every relationship she attempts? Or the one people visit in hospital

Determine today that you're not going to be your own nightmare.

because of self-harming decisions made? Determine today that you're not going to be your own nightmare.

Once you process and shout out the anger (and process you must), preferably in a soundproofed room (you can give full vent to your feelings in there), you can finally take that phone call from Romeo. The same Romeo who has been bellowing at your window every night, forcing the level of intensity to places you're not comfortable with. Finally you can decline his offer, because these days you are the woman who doesn't need to not feel her feelings.

There is a love that you can grab hold of. You can embrace it with a force so powerful that wisdom will be able to do nothing but bow its head. For where love and wisdom submit, there shall you find God.

XIV

'I SHOP AT THE JERKSTORE'

'God hath sworn to lift on high
Who sinks himself by true humility.'

(John Keble)

'I just seem to attract them – jerks that is.'

If I had a cent, a penny or even a monopoly pound, for every time I've overheard this phrase, I'd have funded Disneyland twice over and *bought* every single girl in London a husband. The women using that line feel they can do nothing about this problem. As if they have the same magnetic field as the SG 0418+5729 star*, attracting millions of quoobs*, being swept up in a whirlwind of consequences completely out of their hands, leading to bad hair days, they end up having to arrange sabbaticals for their break-ups.

For complete clarification, by 'jerk' I mean a 'contempt-ibly obnoxious person'. Many memories may plunge to

126

mind when reading this definition. My obvious flashbacks would be the man at the Sanderson lounge bar waving his black AMEX card to get faster service, the man who dumps his girlfriend by text message after discovering a 'female upgrade', the man who insists he must have cod and chips instead of being present at his firstborn's birth. You know, *those* guys – the men who make you want to get a quote for a lobotomy.

So, how do you avoid them in the first place? And how do you attract those steadfast men?

In my learning, I ascertained why I attracted similar traits in men, despite their notable differences in appearance, character and view on life. In short, from the couple of jerks I dated (God bless them!) I learned that they came with a tool belt including the spanner of selfishness, the wrench of pride and a hammer of insensitivity.

I was 18 when I had a cheeky crush on a man, let's call him Warwick. He was a new security guy at the record shop I worked at over the weekends. As always with me, banter began, and there was from the outset a mutual attraction. After only a few meetings, he asked if I wanted to spend some time with him while he manned a building at night. I guess I should have been suspicious when he covered me in a blanket in the back of his car to get through the entrance of the location.

Over the next few weeks, he sent sporadic messages declaring love and heartfelt emotion. I was naive, and smitten. Until one day, after a month of his attention, I took a phone call at the front desk. My friends/colleagues working with me could see my face drop as I listened:

'What's wrong?' they asked, as I put down the phone.

'Just a second,' I responded, dialling the code to make an intercom announcement for the whole of the store to hear.

'This is an announcement for Warwick. Could you come to the front desk, please, your WIFE is on line one.'

My colleagues' faces dropped as much as mine. Running up to the desk, Warwick's expression was one of horror, as he hurriedly whispered, 'I can explain.'

I knew to check in with the obvious details: were they currently married? Or a member of al-Qaeda?

'Oh no no. Your explanation is on line one.' I calmly smiled, as gasps flew around in surround sound while I passed him the phone.

I guess from this moment onwards, I knew to first check the obvious details: were they currently married, or a member of al-Qaeda? I hadn't any idea before this point that men had a capacity to lie for their own gain.

I began to find men of Christian origin by the time I was 26. But my identity in Christ was still fairly shaky. Surely by finally being back in the church I would be able to avoid the jerk species? Oh you're funny.

'I Shop at the Jerkstore'

The church can attract a lot of broken people who are desperate to find the real answers to the meaning of their life. Many find freedom in a determination for spiritual growth, letting go of their pride and surrendering everything to their faith.

Some men (and women) don't carry this through, though. Once they arrive in a church and begin to enjoy that abundance of unconditional love, there's little motivation for them to actually mend their brokenness – because now they've found a place to be accepted despite their mess. The church should love you whether you're healthy or as broken as my 1995 Nintendo Game Boy. When people turn a blind eye to accountability, they are helping those prone towards lethargy in the area of self-development become irresponsible. They place most of the decisions *they* make on God and stunt their emotional maturity in the process.

Such brokenness in a man manifests itself in summing up women like data analysis, getting out the checklists to see if you are right for them – not thinking to check whether they'd be right for you. They often keep back the whole truth – just to keep their options open ready for that 'best choice' that could come any moment. Little do they know this becomes the greatest turn off to healthy, beautiful women.

The quoob isn't direct with himself, keeping you at arm's length but still within reach until he's 'heard from the Lord' or until he's made up his mind to let you go and stop the teasing. But by then the hurt has already been caused. If they had heard from the Lord, then they can't give a flying Gethsemane about your feelings, or they didn't speak to him with your heart in mind in the first place.

If you date this type all the time, forgive my directness here, but the common denominator is you.

This obnoxious element in the jerk dismantles the healthy bonds between brothers and sisters in the church today. When there are no leaders or spiritual fathers to govern the behaviour of young men or the women who play to the teasing, then it's up to us to work out why we were attracted to them in the first place.

I hate to say it, but I will. Women can often attract this volatile emotional dysfunction, maybe for the adventure, or maybe because they've decided he's the best on offer within the stones of the parish. As I've said already, we invite into our lives what we believe we're worth.

If you date this type all the time, forgive my directness here, but the common denominator is you. Your options didn't run out. I understand we are more limited as Christians to find a handsome, thoughtful man to whom God is everything – why do you think I travel?

When I see brilliant single evangelists declaring they want to save ten thousand souls, I whisper advice suggesting they could easily save more than their target margin if men in the church began to treat women for who they really are – daughters of the very King they worship.

For some of us, a pace faster than Usain Bolt is often a reason why we mistakenly took a performance-driven extrovert for a kind-hearted fellow. For others, well we like the attention anyone gives us and, before we know it, we've allowed them to be in our everyday for months. This is where 'falling in love' was a 'fall' – not a conscious choice.

It takes a woman who values herself to believe she deserves the Aston Martins of the Christian dating world – Fiat Puntos just aren't as easy to manoeuvre, nor do they last as long. Fine choices are made outside of a rebound, from of a place of confidence. If you can't handle being single for a time, at least recognize that you are giving a quoob the opportunity to enter and his self-importance to delude you into a false sense of swoon-hood.

It's at this point of no return, the point where you allow God to shape your heart, that men who used to be hidden from your eyes are unveiled to you.

Anne explains, 'Since my divorce, which was deeply damaging, I think I dated men who were compromises because I really didn't think I was worth more. I never make do with second-best cars, clothes, friends, but I have made do with far too many men and ended up hurt and further down the spiral of not thinking I am worth more.'[22]

As you take time each day to focus on God, ignoring what you feel is 'your lack', you will invite honour into your life. I have recently made huge discoveries about the importance of finding a man who loves the Lord so much it would physically hurt his heart to treat you as anything less than the dynamite you are.

It's at this point of no return, the point where you allow God to shape your heart, that men who used to be hidden from your eyes are unveiled to you. God can finally trust you with this breed, knowing you value yourself so much that you won't destroy connection in fear and equally will not tolerate a yo-yo man.

In short, shopping at the jerkstore happens because there is a need to fill a void. In a moment of revelation you will see that, for all the time you were searching for him, you were really searching for *you*.

XV

PANDERING TO
MR POTENTIAL

'There are guys with really high woo and high I,* they come in and can tell you incredible stories about how the Lord is restoring them . . . and it's all flashy and girls get really attracted to that. But there's no foundation, and no depth. There needs to be an ability to recognize history with the Lord and depth that they won't be swayed by every doctrine that comes through the door. Do they have a foundation that will be pointed toward the Lord their entire life?'

(Jake Veach, mentor, pastor, in conversation in 2013)

Dating Mr Potential is a bit like owning a 1957 Mercedes Gullwing. On the occasional drive, it is euphoria at its finest, but, most of the time, you're on the side of the road, with another engine failure and the man from roadside assistance has become your best friend. You had every hope in your investment, but you knew there were risks. As with Mr Abeyant, the pay-off *could* have been incredible, along with the children you'd have had, but those glimpses of him achieving his potential are just that – glimpses.

This, dare I say, has been, to date, my weakest area in relationships. I stand accused and solely admit, that I, Carrie Grace Rebecca Silly Lloyd, have, at times, wanted to rescue men. I subconsciously agreed to take them on enlightening journeys filled with epiphany.

Never fallen in love? Never been sober? Never made amends with your mother? Never expressed your feelings? Can't seem to keep anything enjoyable in your life without sabotaging? No, you're right, it's hard to quit smoking pot when you're a musician, but don't fear! Carrie is here!

And, just like this sentence, Carrie ends up talking in the third person after an astonishing romance story comes to a halt, because she thought she was helping him, never realizing that she actually wanted to change him. Why? Because how he was functioning was horribly unhealthy for those who crossed his path.

Potential is just a word for possibility, and, like all possibilities, they may never come to fruition unless the person in the firing line has the emotional leverage to want to volte-face their actions.

Maybe he tells you he will give up his behaviour with other women. Maybe he does begin to show you his heart is for your retinas only, no one else. The 'give it time' mentality begins to be grateful that you decided to wait, because you can see that he's meaning business with his actions. He didn't just say he was going to change, he actually did.

For three weeks.

Then, true to relapse form, he's gone and done it again. He's covered up inappropriate interaction with a woman and you hear about it on the grapevine. He's back into a selfish realm that you're not allowed to be a part of, unless he invites you.

He's imperfect like you, but if he continues to carry out the same actions that cause the same hurts, why are you staying in the same relationship?

Even though hope is tomorrow's veneer for today's disappointment, it doesn't mean we get to devalue ourselves in the process. He is allowed flaws, he's allowed to get it wrong, he's imperfect like you, but if he continues to carry out the same actions that cause the same hurts, why are you staying in the same relationship? There's a sorry, then there's a repetitive sorry for the same stuff, girlfriend. It indicates a lack of teachability. And you're sweeter, sharper, than that.

This is where you need to consider if you're going to help yourself to rise above it all. Women who seek to fix others, have a need to fix themselves first. Even though hope is the motivation for why everything is done on the planet, hope in the wrong place, at the wrong time, for the wrong person officially stops your destiny's momentum.

This propensity for hope in a man is a brilliant talent in marriage, but it's a dating detriment before covenant. As Jon Van Epp says, 'In marriage, the persevering forces of attachment and commitment are essential to overcoming challenges partners face. But in a dating relationship, the stronger your feelings of affinity and loyalty, the more likely you will overlook shortcomings and failures in partners . . . encouraging serious problem areas that should be addressed once they are exposed.'[23]

I've seen the benefit of every doubt in my time, including real humdingers such as: 'He's charming and our connection is incredible,' 'He always apologizes for his drinking if he has said something untoward. He's working on it,' 'Oh but depression helps with his songwriting' and even 'he's so misunderstood, only I know the real him.'

So when they do become sober, you'd think this is where dating Mr Potential ends, and dating Mr Awesomeness begins? Not necessarily. Because he's still working out how to be whole, just like you.

I finished a two-and-a-half-year relationship with a man whose incredible talent to drink a bottle of brandy in one evening became a little heady. He would turn up to auditions drunk, and by the afternoon he'd begin to shake if he hadn't downed a shot. He'd preface the morning after with tears and remorseful apologies. I'd forgive him – only to be confronted by his 4 p.m. Smirnoff face. Months later, after the break-up, he'd woo me back with a newfound sobriety.

Thinking the drink was in the past, I took him back. He stayed sober, but the scourings of low self-esteem were still there and it was that which propelled the drinking problem in the first place – not the taste of a fine liquor. I stayed for a few more months, but the jaws of his insecurities had eaten up my fight. And of course in the months to come, after forgiveness and healing, I wondered why I had stayed for the entire length of the showdown rather than getting out earlier.

It's not your job to lead them into a healthier existence. It's not your job to disciple anyone you love into a greater sense of identity.

There comes a place in our lives where, amongst all the wistful hope, we have to be realistic. It's not your job to lead them into a healthier existence. It's not your job to disciple anyone you love into a greater sense of identity.

When I've prayed over these types of relationships, the ones where I've been taken in by their charm, ignoring quite important ailments, I've asked the Lord what I should do. Every time he's replied:

Carrie, please leave this to me.

As Christians we believe it's our duty to introduce others to the light – so often we become high-handed, tyrannical in approach. You believe you're doing him a favour by pointing out his issues. Am I right? The good news is you can exert your power over yourself, but you can't exert your power over him. Welcome to free will.

Just like Jesus with Judas, you cannot change Mr Potential. I repeat. You cannot change him. I've seen brilliant men recognize the problems that impound everyone else, but still refuse to look at their own issues. If they don't want to look in the box, they won't look in the box. No attempts to make them jealous or wearing a tighter skirt, is going to win them around. If it does, your man will be easily manipulated by anyone, at any time. Don't you need a man who will take responsibility for their own self-development?

There is liberation in understanding this. Threatening to finish the relationship in the hope he'll change, or leaving with the false hope that he'll fight for you, is energy much more worthy of spending on non-profit charities like Amnesty International or The Red Cross, to name two.

You want to stop dating Mr Potential? Look at what he is right now, and keep your eyes on your goal. Don't make that particular man your destination, because he wasn't your goal before he came into your life. Your goal was to have a healthy relationship in which a man honours you, leads you but also allows you to lead, lets your voice be heard, isn't intimidated by you, covers you and fights for teamwork above his own desires.

You can insert the name into that goal later, just know this – it should never be complicated. The right relationship needn't fight too hard to rest in love.

Be flexible, but never hold on to false hope. If you do, you'll fall in love with a person that doesn't exist, a man you invented in the very desires of your own imagination, packaged in the delectable image of your boyfriend.

Besides, Mr Steadfast (who has a desire to grow) will be happy you didn't fight for Mr Potential. Because Mr Steadfast will overtake Mr Potential and take you on a journey you never dreamt of. Even better, Mr Steadfast will instigate damage control immediately if he's done anything to hurt you, ensuring you're not hurt by the same action again.

Get out of Mr Potential's driving seat, let him and God do the fixing, and go ahead and enjoy the presence of great men who exist in this world right now. We were never meant to mould men into something they are not. Valiant men do that solely of their own accord.

We were never meant to mould men into something they are not. Valiant men do that solely of their own accord.

'Those who trust their own insight are foolish, but anyone who walks in wisdom is safe' (Proverbs 28:26, NLT). So if you do desire to have a man at some point in your incredible destiny, then be on the lookout for Mr Steadfast, for he listens to God first, conversing with his heart and head in unison. Don't be swayed by charm, for it's as fleeting as a storm and as stable as a one-hit wonder.

CARRIE'S PRACTICAL POINTERS

- **It is harder for Christian women in this age to find men not just of faith but who are sons, lovers and servants.** If they are not in your community, use your air miles! Travel abroad if you must. There is revival breaking out everywhere, so go find the hunger and suffocate fear's voice.
- Pace is crucial for the health of dating. No one need be mentioning marriage from week one unless you've been good friends for a while. **Whoever is going at the slower pace – that is your guide.** Ask yourself why your foot is on the throttle. Any quiet manipulation shown in this process doesn't honour them as a child of God.
- Freedom is key in union. Co-dependency is rife as it is focused on self-gratification. If you are not growing, or one of you is intimidated by the other person's growth, self-sabotage will occur. These relationships scar if you're not careful. You are not there to fix them – **you should be with someone because you like who they are as a person, not because they hold the answer for you.**
- **Relationships can be easy and needn't involve too**

much fight before covenant. If you're expecting them to emulate the behaviour of your friend's husband he, remember, is just your boyfriend; the other made a covenant vow and is *expected* to work and fight harder for his wife. **Your guy must be allowed to make mistakes – it's how he fixes them that indicates whether he is a keeper.**

- Attracting jerks? Why are you intrigued by charmers who are treating your heart poorly? Why is drama and chaos more attractive than love? Self-value? Believe that you don't deserve the full attention? **Get honest friends to be real with you, get humble and be excited – you're about to see your desires for men change.** Research healthy men. What virtues do they have? Take notes. Then start with yourself in the restoration process.

- Everyone has potential, but is your ideal of your man delusional, and reality never enough for you? Don't seek perfection, but rather a teachable heart. Not that it is for you to teach him – no. Does he sit down with God, seeking more wisdom within his own intimate relationship?

PART IV

SEX ON, SEX OFF

The battle of the burning loins is being made even more tempestuous in the most sexualized society to date. Wherever you walk, there is an opinion on the subject – whether it's sinful, whether it's liberating. So what are we Christian ladies to do with the modern approach to all game and no holding back? As we steward our hearts to be healthy, so must this subject be discussed in order to steward the entire relationship with Kingdom values. If we're going to do this, if we're going to believe the Bible for all it's worth, then we can't ignore parts to satiate our desires. We are wired in physical ways that cannot be denied. It's time to change our approach to sexuality within a Christian culture, to understand that sex is a wonderful thing, as long as it remains harmless to others and is contextualized for abundant glory.

XVI

FIGHTING FOMO*

> 'Self-respect is the fruit of discipline; the sense of dignity
> grows with the ability to say no to oneself.'
> (Abraham Joshua Heschel)

Let's cut to the chase: do we miss out by not having sex before marriage?

Just as my school nurse would blame a sprained ankle on a girl's monthly period, so too did my school-mates blame my unwillingness to have sex with acne-ridden 15-year-olds on my 'wimpish fear'.

My reluctance to lose my virginity at school was so well known that one kid wanted to profile me in the school gazette. A bit harsh, I thought, especially as they said they needed something to fill the sports section.

In 1995, Britain sent its forces to join the longest siege of a capital city in the history of modern warfare (Sarajevo), unemployment was on the rise and the Queen Mother had had a rather traumatic hip operation, but, most importantly, Carrie Lloyd, from year 12, wouldn't 'put out'. To my schoolmates it had become a national tragedy. A bit like when Ross cheated on Rachel with that photocopier chick in *Friends*.

Such ribbing can happen when one's lifestyle isn't matching that of *The Full Monty* or *Pulp Fiction*. I preferred singing along to Julie Andrews prancing about on that hilltop in *The Sound of Music* (she was clearly helicoptered in), than watching Uma Thurman get stabbed in the chest with an intracardiac injection. But some people had an issue with my preferences.

> 'Maybe Margaret is a tiger in the bedroom. You don't know. And, might I add, it wasn't her "ride 'em cowboy" sex life that won us the Falklands war.'

Of course the words 'frigid', 'uptight' and 'about as much fun as Margaret Thatcher' were spurted around in my home economics class.

I had witty quips ready to contest such Marge jokes:

'Maybe Margaret is a tiger in the bedroom. You don't know. And, might I add, it wasn't her "ride 'em cowboy" sex life that won us the Falklands war.'

Still my stigma grew. Even the teachers got involved . . .

'Miss, why do I appear to have only got a D on my natural science paper?' I'd ask my Physics teacher.

146

'That's probably because you're a virgin.'

They were all in on it.

Even when I delivered a speech to my class, fundraising for the Leprosy Mission, recounting stories of how the patients would not notice scalding themselves when carrying hot pans due to the disease, I was interrupted by one of the class 'highlights' (bullies):

'How can lepers carry saucepans without fingers?'

Silence.

'Is this because I've never had sex?' I asked.

I missed the simpler days of being 13, when the only obsessions my girlfriends had were the newly invented Venus Lady Shave and how to arabesque on ice skates. But a new season of self-sabotage had become the rage; amphetamines, drinking cider 'til you could puke and learning all the lyrics to Cypress Hill's *Black Sunday* album (can they construct a sentence without a swear word?) were *the* things to be doing in your spare time.

I had contemplated involving myself in some friends' recreational activities one night, when one of them piped up with a revelatory idea:

'Let's see how many ecstasy tablets we can take tonight!'

A few of her friends excitedly clapped their hands, until I responded:

'Until what? – *death*?'

By university, I fell into surprising odds when 65 per cent of the year in my performing arts school were gay musical theatre wannabes. It was the best of times – and the best of times. No longer were straight men standing behind me in nightclubs repeating 'He's not going to wait for marriage, neither will he . . . nor he.' Instead my camp-as-Christmas friends would fight over who was going to take the part of Louisa for *The Sound of Music*. *Dirty Dancing's* 'I've Had the Time Of My Life' was performed in every bar – the ones that hadn't already banned us from practising the jumping splits off the beer pumps that is.

I belonged, finally.

By my early twenties, I was dating an actor in London's *Blood Brothers*. He knew how to romance. Every two weeks he would travel seven hours on a bus from London to Liverpool, fill up my fridge with food (student living lacked such luxuries), but one day he left a card on the counter saying, 'I love you so much. P.S. Most people would be having sex by now.'

Mother Teresa had a different focus. 'Yes that's it,' I thought to myself. 'I'll get a career. Then when I'm rich, or a saint, people will wait for as long as I tell them to.'

Naturally I vaporized the relationship and, in my mourning, learnt the routine to Michael Jackson's 1995 MTV Music Awards performance. After all, as I kept reminding myself: 'Who needs a manipulative boyfriend when you have male friends who don't care if you give in to peer pressure because they find you as sexually attractive as Marilyn Manson?'

By now, however, I was beginning to feel like my rights for holding out for my wedding night were becoming a little jaded. Was I completely insane? I had no Christian community, no Christian Union to remind me of why purity protects the soul, instead of draining it. I had no church to go to, no one my age. The stark commentary I was hearing every day was making it apparent I may never marry if I didn't have sex.

Mother Teresa had a different focus. 'Yes, that's it,' I thought to myself, 'I'll get a career. Then when I'm rich, or a saint, people will wait for as long as I tell them to.'

I found that, probably because my V-plates were still apparent, just like my high school friends, university buddies would come to me in confidence about their sexual experiences. For them, I was the safe one who couldn't give an opinion – just a hug and maybe a quiet jig to a Bob Fosse track.

When I was younger, before this all began, I heard stupidly in-love married couples share about the wonders of sex. I wanted that. The cherished, committed, I-am-not-going-to-leave-you-for-a-36DD-woman-called-Pearl-next-week, type of sex. THAT'S what I wanted. Stories of spiritual encounters in the bedroom between two marrieds were utterly enthralling when it came to covenant. Angelic encounters, a presence of the Holy Spirit on the wedding night, a deepening of connection that can only happen in that union were tales I read about, but no icons as such were breathing anywhere near me.

On the flip side, back at '*Fame* school', I endured conversations like this:

'He will only have sex if we play Coldplay. Particularly the song "Fix You",' or, 'You won't understand this Carrie, but sometimes I just don't want to do it. But s/he insists. I just want to kick back with a Sudoku puzzle but, if I don't comply, they start calling up their other boyfriend/girlfriend.'

My FOMO (fear of missing out) was actually FOBER (fear of being rejected). I'll not lie, I suffered privately at times when I wasn't able to be around my nonchalant gay friends; nights where I'd cry myself to sleep after one too many self-deprecating jokes in a day. I would write in my virgin journal, wear my virgin pyjamas and chat with Sam, my musical teddy bear, the only other virgin I could talk to. Even though I had great friends I was as misunderstood as the Rubik's Cube and utterly confused by the barrage of opinions that told me I should do everything in my power to ruin myself through drugs, drinking and a lot of sex.

I should have been as proud as punch with my decision but, after twenty-three years, I was beginning to question why I was holding on.

This was the reason why I stopped considering marriage in my twenties. I assumed everyone would grow out of this incessant desire to lose their virginity once they learnt it's not the gateway to adulthood as they had hoped. Or they just really wanted to have sex, for their raging hormones were screaming too loudly. But regardless, I hoped that they might get a little more choosy about their bedroom partners, simply so I didn't have to watch so many tears flood their dormitories during the break-ups.

I lost my virginity somewhere in between falling in love with a handsome Muslim, who told me he would wait, and the sudden death of my father.

Losing my virginity really wasn't a conscious decision, more a response to my broken need to be loved now my entire world (my dad) had been snatched away from me. I no longer had anyone to value myself for. Dad would remind me of my beauty and my worth, while advising on my boyfriends with an 'approve or deny' regime.

I fell sucker to a lie that giving my entire being to a man who 'was different', because he had said he would wait, could result in my 'I've finally given a man satisfaction' itch being scratched.

The feeling of fulfilment didn't last long for me. I lived in a fog for months, repeating the same action, all the while mourning the fact that I had fought the battlefield for virginity for this long only to give in and to have sex this way. It was at this point in my life where the FOMO really came to town.

I couldn't hear from God any more.

I'd speak to God but get no response. Not like before. Unlike the times in which I could almost tangibly touch his presence, now I'd sense nothing but empty air. I'd walk around in a daze of conviction thinking, 'I've messed with my Dad, and he's not talking to me.' Of course this wasn't the case – God hadn't packed up and left my apartment block.

I realized I hadn't been missing out on anything – just propaganda. I did miss God, however. By my late twenties I claimed back my desire for purity after falling in love with God.

Misplacing my sexuality didn't mean I was going directly to the burning pits of hell. The enemy's attempt at spiritual warfare through my own body had won. I had come into agreement with something loveless. My fight for purity was eroded the moment I couldn't find a reason to continue. Remember, I had no personal relationship with God at this age, so had no desire to protect his heart.

The enemy's agenda is to demolish everything heaven wants to raise up.

When I became an atheist in my mid-twenties, I was having sex. No, I didn't take ecstasy until death (obviously), yet the FOMO became worse. The satisfaction, the belonging, the 'being the same', became much more dissatisfactory. Not because sex was terrible and, as I had no conscience for conviction, little shame cropped up, but sex wasn't the gateway to the eternal love I had once hoped it would be.

That desire to love and be loved in abundance kept hounding me.

I realized I hadn't been missing out on anything – just propaganda. I did miss God, however. By my late twenties I claimed back my desire for purity after falling in love with God. It wasn't until I had a real relationship with him as my Father that conviction came home to my heart and I finally corrected my errors. It was tough to turn my back on sex, knowing how dynamic it can be, but I wasn't tempted to do it this side of walking down the aisle. It wasn't worth the exchange of God.

Nothing ever is.

Society might have had its trends of reckless self-gratification. And in the moments I wasn't joining in, it seemed like I was missing out, but with my 20/20 hindsight, peer pressure was only mounted because my moral compass caused others to question the direction of their own path. Such a difference can be uncomfortable for a peer to palate. I only wish I'd gripped onto self-value just a few years earlier because I've never felt more free than I do right now.

Today, as I write this in the Hollywood hills of Los Angeles, billboards of breasts and bums scatter the skyline telling me what I should feel. But the motivation behind them all is always money, self-gratification and, again, money.

The heavens overlooking me right now are only ever motivated to endorse self-control and sacrifice for one thing – love. It is for this reason that I never want to argue again with the very creator of the orgasm.

For, so far, I've never missed out on anything when I've listened to him.

XVII

IS THERE FUN WITHOUT FORBIDDEN FRUIT?

'Tasting what could have been – what should have been – didn't make it easier.'

(Kele Moon, *Beyond Eden*)

'According to our stats, we wouldn't get along, but we would have fantastic sex.'

This was a *real* message from a random man sent to my friend, while she was frequenting the world of online dating. My response to her followed thus:

'Girl, I think you should reply with this message: "Kind Sir, How polite of you to get in touch despite our personality clash. If we were not to get on, I doubt I would want to have sexual intercourse with you. This, in turn, would make it unnecessary rape. And there's nothing like a bit of rape to break the formalities of introductions. Kindest regards, Miss 'Dodged a Bullet' . . .'"

In the twenty-first century the man's message is considered standard conversational dating banter. To suggest at this point that you plan to avoid having sex before marriage is downright scandalous. 'Where's the fun in that?' is the usual response as they down their Wild Turkey at lightning speed.

I've chewed the forbidden fruit and it didn't care for my wellbeing.

Equally we've seen those virgin bride shows that result in me throwing my Bible at the television screen; virgins who have been so pure in their journey that they've still not had sex two years *after* marriage. Picture the scene: the poor husband is having a cold shower in case he should experience 'naughty bedroom thoughts' while his wife is calming herself by eating a raw sweet potato. And so, my life is often categorized by others as being part of the sweet potato brigade – a pageant I have no intention of partnering with.

For me, well I've chewed the forbidden fruit and it didn't care for my wellbeing. I'm referring to the three sexual relationships I had from the age of 23 until a few years ago, when I decided to hang up my Agent Provocateur negligees, the contraceptive pill and my need to perform for requited love with the cunning use of my thighs.

Is There Fun Without Forbidden Fruit?

This chapter isn't going to augment the warning label on sex before marriage. It doesn't help the Millennial generation to hear about the bitter cup any more. They've heard it for decades. They know that HPV can cause cervical cancer, that syphilis is coming back with a vengeance (something to share in common with Hitler and Beethoven), that an attachment hormone called 'oxytocin' becomes active in the system after sexual interaction, which can distort emotional rationale in choosing the perfect mate to wed.

The message of purity came as damnation threats to govern control, rather than creating an attractive branded advertising campaign.

We know the statistics. We've seen the rise in teenage pregnancy in the last two decades. We've met the love-childs from the 1960s free lovers (if the women hadn't already given paper notes in an envelope to some dodgy Harley Street doctor to perform an illegal abortion). We've heard the cautionary nightmares handed to us by our parents, teachers, mentors and, let's not forget, Saint Oprah.

Our (the church's) approach to sex before marriage hasn't been healthy over the years. The message of purity came as damnation threats to govern control, rather than creating an attractive branded advertising campaign. After all, sex sells – purity doesn't, unless you are buying a book on how to stop your loins from burning pre-marriage.

From the stories of storks delivering babies, to hideous pictures of herpes in school classrooms, one extreme avoids the topic, the other attempts to build fear amidst our inner desire that wants to, at some point, have sex with someone we love.

In the 1950s the word 'bottom' was not to be printed in *Woman* magazine. Witnessing your parents hugging was completely taboo. This prudish approach caused a disconnection with their children. The sexually charged backlash instigated the sixties' sexual revolution: Woodstock, the mini-skirt, LSD, The Rolling Stones and a propensity for 'trying anything' took over.

BREAKING NEWS: we're naturally wired with desires. Suggesting suppression of these is where we've gone a little loo-lah.

Suppression of these often causes revolt and strict law will always invite a desperate need for freedom. When people do things out of a sense of duty to the law, often they plan to break out or seek escape. When you do things for the love of others and yourself, and therefore for God, there are certainly less tears.

Discipline, at one time, meant strict suppressive fathers with no listening ear and the personality of Johnny Cash. The wrathful God of the Old Testament seemed so distant to me; I had zilch relationship with him and the religious approach in churches only reinforced my fear of joyless judgement with no room for questions.

Is There Fun Without Forbidden Fruit?

I've got friends who, alongside myself, had 'choosy sex' (sex with those whom we were in long-term committed relationships with) in happy relationships, with no pregnancy alarms or trips to the health clinic. When they broke up from their partners they were still quite happy about the intimacy shared. Warning labels of STDs, even oxytocin fears, have not been argument enough to justify purity. Fear of consequences is an argument, but it rarely convinces those getting their kicks from playtime. Sex is powerful, so reasoning through fear tactics is futile.

This will be controversial for some, but for those that aren't interested in God, if you want to have sex before covenant, no one is stopping you and no one should condemn you – just as no one should condemn me for moving away from pre-marital sex.

Remaining pure is a battle because our brains have been designed by God to have intimacy.

Right now, I'm addressing the ones who want to delve into the entire essence of God, who want to have relationships that are more meaningful than lust, karma sutra, upside-down antics and diaphragms. This is about honouring how phenomenal sex is and, therefore, not messing with it.

Remaining pure is a battle because our brains have been designed by God to have intimacy, to have that orgasmic connection with another person. God is not a 'system', he has created you to experience insatiable pleasure. The more we dally in casual sexual lifestyles, the more we miss the opportunity for human connection on God-designed ecstatic levels. We end up 'creating' a God to whom we go to, to beg for what we want, never quite understanding that perhaps the Lord kept sex for covenant for a reason other than a fear of contracting HIV.

Where the sixties revolution stopped inspiring me (Twiggy, Warhol and Jimmy Hendrix aside) was this belief that doing whatever you want, whenever you want it, backed by the 'free love' mantra, excused a lot of behaviour that left women crying (post-coitus) in strangers' bedrooms, with no idea of how to say no. Sixties wild-child, columnist Virginia Ironside wrote an article reflecting this era:

'After a decade of sleeping around pretty indiscriminately, girls of the sixties eventually became fairly jaded about sex. It took me years to discover that continual sex with different partners is, with very few exceptions, joyless, uncomfortable and humiliating, and it's only now I'm older that I've discovered that one of the ingredients of a good sex life is, at the very least, a grain of affection between the two partners involved.'[24]

'A grain of affection,' you say? I liked her honesty. After all, the sixties revolution created free lust, not love. And all lust does is devalue the power of sex.

From that decade onwards, the standard of morality – saving sex for the man who made a commitment to fight for and to love us for the rest of our lives, became a preposterous idea, not an honourable one. Sexual freedom created a supply and demand rollercoaster. When I say no to a man, he just finds it elsewhere, needing to do very little to obtain it. But when I say no, I'm doing my girls a service, creating a standard that not only protects me but other women too. If I say yes, I'm not just abusing the value I have of myself, I'm abusing the chances of other girls getting great men, as I set a lower standard of what it looks like to fight for a woman of worth.

Oh, don't get me wrong, lust can be spontaneously exhilarating – but it doesn't make people feel known. And I want to be known. My sexuality can mask the real me, and the real them.

Do we miss out on enjoyment, amusement and pleasure if we cut out sex and all its surrounding activities? The question misses the point. We lose that experience of being read outside the bedroom. We are able to give in to all the desires and get our needs met. But what we lose if we give in to those physical urges is the greatest loss of all. If we gain more intimacy than the level of trust we might have for the other person, what else do we have to base relationship on? An ability to hold the Firefly pose in yoga?

Inside of covenant, sex is the greatest weapon to destroy the enemy's work. Outside of covenant, sex is the greatest weapon to destroy *me*. That's the accuser's aim. He knows that if I have sex, I'll do an awful lot to do it again, and again.

161

The power sex creates between two people, skin on skin, knocks any other connection out of the water. The accuser sees how powerful it is and, because he can't create anything, he can only distort sex into being 'fun' without love. And this will destroy someone's heart at some point of the game. Denying its prepollence doesn't stop the power, it just causes more damage.

God called us to be free. Freedom means loving each other, not placing us above them for self-gain. Freedom gives, with consideration. Freedom treasures, without destruction. Freedom doesn't look like one-night stands. It isn't fearful. It isn't the walk of shame. It is not the tears into your pillow because he didn't call. It isn't the break-up after the intimacy exceeded the trust. It isn't manipulation of sexy kicks. It isn't Sex Addicts Anonymous. It isn't porn. Freedom values a purity so rich in its taste that anything else can't be swallowed.

After seven years of being in a few sexual relationships and other relationships that were 'pure', I saw a familiar pattern that built up more fear of abandonment than fun and less connection with God – and therefore myself.

I was chucking diamonds to men and they were losing their worth. Giving my body to a boy who did love me created a connection on many levels. But it was futile without spiritual connections, without authorization from the very inventor of sex.

'Oh here we go,' I can feel some liberal lovers respond. What some don't understand, and what many believers attempt to work their way *around*, is that the relationship with God is what gets affected the most. If we don't fight for God, we don't fight for love.

My friend Ruth Atkins told me, 'When I got saved, I left my lifestyle of sex, but I needed a better reason than "God said don't do it". He showed me that the best sex is worth fighting for.'[25]

Ruth's comment reveals the main reason why so many Christians do hold out – it's why I changed my behaviour. However, women were married at 14 in biblical times. They weren't 30, waiting much longer for marriage, and often that's why purity baffles even Christians in the church.

'Oh I wouldn't have sex with him unless I was willing to have children with him,' I used to say, thinking that was the responsible approach. I, and many others like me, justified the exploratory encounters in the bedroom with the abundance of the grace of God, who will love us no matter what. And often we truly believed what we told ourselves, 'We will be married. In time. When he's ready.'

My value of the apple surpassed my value of what I really wanted, which was to be understood, valued and covered. It's what most people want, isn't it?

These days I embellish the tiny moments. Avoiding christianese here, I do like it when a guy prays with me. When he emotionally expresses affirmation. When he honours me exclusively rather than eyeing up other women. When he tells me he won't ever be satisfied with just my body. When he self-sacrifices my soul sings. I feel a physical warmth when I feel known by a man who will fight for me, protect me and my sexuality – and has done so out of choice.

Fun isn't found in the forbidden fruit, it's found in picking the finest fruit, at the best time, with the approval of the master gardener.

The question is not: Is there fun without forbidden fruit? The question is: Is fun more important to you than loving others triumphantly and loving God more intimately?

Let's not mess with weapons of mass destruction. For outside of marriage there is nothing but war wounds, scars from shrapnel and a distorted view of men taking advantage of women (or perhaps vice versa) who were always meant to be celebrated and held in the highest esteem. We must also celebrate and allow men to be the powerful sons God called them to be, who can save the most intimate act ever created, between two people who have more than a grain of affection for each other, laying down their lives, through thick and thin.

Awaken your soul to the counter-cultural concept of empowering sex in its pricelessness once more. As we ensure the stock value in covenant sex rises, therein lies the crown to the throne of merriment.

XVIII

MAKE LOVE, NOT PORN

'But I say to you that everyone who looks at a woman with lustful intent has already committed adultery with her in his heart.'

(Matthew 5:28, ESV)

When *GQ* magazine released their article '10 Reasons Why You Should Quit Watching Porn', everyone rubbed their eyes and re-read the title. Surely *GQ* were the first ones to write an article titled '10 Reasons Why You Should Dump Your Girlfriend and Click Online'? Isn't it mandatory for them to print the sexiest women wearing nothing but a man's white shirt with hints of skin on every other page?

You know there's an issue when such a magazine controversially opposes that which society has accepted into the 'tolerate' bracket. You know we're going too far when

David Cameron restricts the internet from the British nation's pornographic fingertips.

Once I began to abstain from sex in my last sexual relationship, I still continued to love/date the guy – he was very, very understanding (poor guy didn't have much choice, although I guess he could have left) and I still had desires for him. I turned to pornography to stave off any temptation towards him and even sent him the links to check it out himself. I didn't want him feeling powerless.

All was well. Until soft pornography needed to be a little more graphic, a little more rough around the edges, less of a story, less chit chat, more people and, before I knew it, only after a few months – enough to claim a habit – I was watching stuff that you'd scream at should you stumble upon it in the flesh. When it came to a girl being subjected by one too many men, I caught myself speaking out, 'WHAT IN HELL'S NAME AM I WATCHING?'

My desensitization could be put down to what neuroscientists would call opening new neural pathways, inducing an orgasm from visually pornographic images. This Pavlovian approach is self-serving and the sexual images pervasive. It does not encourage *eros** but, instead, dissolves it. In short, this approach says, 'I don't care if your sexual parts belong to you any more, or that they do anything for you, I care about what it all does for me.'

Men and women often seek help from therapists with their marriages when the screen has gained more attention than the spouse. When your sex drive is dictated by the puppet master of pornography you've lost control of what even inspires you any more. Those of us who've succumbed don't believe we need intimacy when we have porn, but the irony is that porn makes you feel lonelier when you've switched it off.

In tests, a porn addict's brain scan shows brain waves no different to that of a crack addict, according to Cambridge students. And with almost 50 per cent of porn users never having had sex in the real world, with real people,[26] then we have a problem: they've already shot any chance of real intimacy with any potential marriage partner in the face.

So many of us have believed the lie that porn doesn't harm anyone and it's just a little sexual kick, nothing to worry about. That is, until you look your man in the eyes and realize something has changed. You're no longer rendered breathless by a look from him, and you're not happy until he's been almost violent with you. When he or you have been stimulated by different images, all of a sudden your sexual desires are very different to each other; the URL has become more powerful than your connection. Before you know it, the enemy is brushing off his hands and crawling away; another relationship down the pan. And if he can get into their brains before boys and girls even meet anyone to fall in love with, even better.

I've never taken drugs, because I knew it would open up an experience that would make me want to go back to it again and again. If I'm ignorant as to how drugs make you feel, then even better. I needn't go down that road and can still have a great time without them, because I know nothing else. I didn't realize that porn could have the same addictive affect.

Ted Bundy took one look at a single pornographic image as a kid and, although not everyone will end up being executed as a necrophile, it only takes one seed for it to grow. The power of porn is not to be overlooked.

Erica Greve, founder of Unlikely Heroes, told me: 'There is a growing body of research that looks at the correlation between violent pornography and the increase in violent male sexual behaviour. Does that mean that all men who watch violent pornography will rape a woman? Of course not. However, most men who rape attest that they are users of violent pornography.'

For as long as porn is the main go-to for a man (or woman) to feel powerful, the relationship faces damage.

To give another example, a very well-respected head teacher delved into soft porn during some problems in his marriage. He viewed it as 'light fun' to experience a form of freedom from the powerlessness he was feeling, without having sex. Two years later he found himself in prison, having been caught with child pornography. A place he never anticipated experiencing.

It's no different to me puffing on a Marlboro, and as a 15-year-old kid asks me if I have one to spare I reply, 'You don't wanna start kid. It'll only cost you money – then your life. Now go and play hopscotch.'

It's not worth risking what your brain could start to get its high from, never mind making you think about nothing else. The more I counsel friends, relationships and readers of Her Glass Slipper, the more I see the damage porn causes. For as long as porn is the main go-to for a man (or woman) to feel powerful, the relationship faces damage. Some marriages I know about were willing to work through the porn addiction, while some gave up, finalizing their divorce, and to this day the addicted partners seek someone that can sexually fulfil them; a futile dream that often only leads to more isolation, depression and loneliness.

All porn addiction is one giant scream to the world that the person involved doesn't feel known.

Louis Theroux explored the porn industry in one documentary, revisiting years later to find that some stars had committed suicide or turned to prostitution to make ends meet and one had made more adult films to cope with the death of a baby.

People don't turn to porn when they're happy, they turn to it when they're lonely or misunderstood.

As I have seen wives or husbands come off sex chat rooms, exit fetish clubs or turn down the offer of high class orgies disguised as 'classy stately home masquerade parties', I have been told that their sexual functions improved. Relationships found connection again. Some even felt fully loved for the very first time.

I would suggest that women who become porn artists sign on the dotted line. They agreed to partake in the industry, so to say that we dehumanize them isn't right because, for the most part, it was really their choice. But then there are the side businesses that gain income from the residue of the sex industry, and this was where I saw a whole other perspective.

When I came face to face with young victims of sex trafficking, my view on porn changed. I saw that, not only was it a relationship buster, demonic in its aim, but porn is connected to sex trafficking. The porn producers stretched the limits of sexual exploration and visual images to pig vomit or live worms, desensitizing their own perspective to trivialize paedophilia and place it in this same game. All at the abuse and expense of girls too young, too emotionally vulnerable.

Economic decline and international transportation were merely additional help that made South East Asia one of the most plagued parts of the developing world for sex trafficking. As I travelled there I saw girls crying in front of me, who were being raped night after night, for $4. I said

$4. For the price you paid for this book, you could have had four girls looking no older than 12, to do whatever you wanted with them.

Again, Erica shared with me: 'I remember walking down the street in Pattaya, Thailand, and seeing a beautiful, young, scantily clad Thai girl walking down the street with a very unattractive, almost gruesome-looking Western man. Pattaya is the sex tourism capital of the world, and many tourists go to Pattaya to solicit sex from the girls forced to work in the bars and brothels. The young Thai girl was doing what most women would have a difficult time doing . . . she was hanging on the man's every word, gaze locked, laughing and giggling at his every movement. What struck me from this encounter was that for probably around $4, this troubled man had done the unthinkable – he had won the undeserved gaze of a beautiful young girl for which he had not paid the price of relationship, marriage or even self-development. His $4 in Thailand had bought him the same thing that $4 buys a man watching porn . . . for that brief moment he feels powerful.'

Heartburn got the better of me as I watched Western men in Manila airport on their phones, booking their next destination – the bars. You think paedophiles are a rarity? Think again. There are thousands of them that can get their live sex kicks thanks to the cunning inspiration of bad story lines, baby oil and a home video camera.

Searching deeper, friends from around the globe have emailed me stories, the worst case being when a friend had managed to record a phone conversation with another man who was the evil negotiator seeking to kidnap children from Russian orphanages and sell them on. As my friend witnessed and trialled for the UN, he saw pictures of 18-month-old bodies that had died from internal bleeding, due to rape. All culprits had watched porn.

One click on one of these websites and, just like the ignorant pot users that buy a tiny amount of dope to get high once in a while, porn addicts involve themselves in the chain of events that allow a business to exceed trillions in revenue, costing our governments millions to eradicate its side effects – murder, rape, sexually diseased death and kidnapping. You think porn doesn't harm anyone? Wake up and come out from the duvet of denial you've been hiding under.

Don't think because you've watched a free preview online that lasted no longer than five minutes that your keypad is clean of crime. The history of your computer stays in the abyss of the internet. You can't backspace your mind and you can't backspace your computer. You're playing with fire and no one is there to extinguish your thoughts.

When dealing with the pimps themselves, you don't understand just how evil they can be. One of my girlfriends, Melissa, who found the insurmountable love of

Christ in jail after being involved in sex-trafficking rings for a few years, told me that when one guy proposed the idea of her working for him, he sat her down at a table and warned: 'You do know I'm the devil, don't you?'

Pimps have no problem throwing girls onto the streets with the ugliest of STDs, making them homeless and deeming them 'no use' by the time they're 15. They have no consciences. They have no desire for anything other than to rip the souls from the women and sell them for meat.

My friend talked about the effects that porn had on her clients, making them less human, more monsters. The more they built porn into their daily life, the more they had no problem with calling her number.

Sometimes the men would make a performance of it in front of each other; the bravado made them feel powerful, if just for thirty minutes. Until one evening, a bunch of military boys had hired her for the night – with one man who was much more reserved. Bashful, almost, he really didn't want to partake in what was happening. He showed concern for her, cared all of a sudden for what was beneath the packaging. But something got in the way for her: 'If God had wanted to bring in a man to show me true intimacy and love, I wouldn't have been able to receive it.'

Like all beautiful God-like moments, she shares her story with a turnaround of events that shows just how stunning

God's grace and love is. Today she leads a life of wanting to love herself above all. Abstinence from porn had to be a part of the recovery from that industry:

'The practical bodily restoration that you have to do, you have to want it and you have to work on it. It puts the responsibility back on you. A lot of people don't want to take ownership and they will find any spiritual reason to get what they want. No. You have to take responsibility for you and your own soul ties*.'

What you invest in is where you find your life. Distorted views of sex will make you feel powerful in the moment, but just as the antonym of the word 'power' is 'impotence', so too will the exploration into that world make you finally impotent to find freedom. Porn is a trap behind closed doors that literally brainwashes humans into believing they're getting their kicks from strangers having sex.

Many of us fall for porn in a bad patch, when the soul is dehydrated. We drink and drink, and yet are still thirsty.

Evil cloaks sex in lust, hoping we will mistake it for freedom. Many of us fall for porn in a bad patch, when the soul is dehydrated. We drink and drink, and yet are still thirsty. The thirst is not quenched. Those who have fallen into the addictive grip have been poisoned with more lies, detaching the physical from the emotional. However powerful you believe porn to be, it's up to you if you want to sign up. But consider: does porn bring you life? Or does it bring a slow death? To the world? To your lover? Most importantly, to you?

XIX

THE SEX-SLIP

'It's not the action that makes me ponder so much as why I did it in the first place, when within my heart I had no plan to?'

(Journal entry, 2011)

If you make the 'sex-slip', that 'oh crap what have I done' moment – whether it's sex before marriage or a physical encounter that left you more breathless than it should – there is no Tippex for the error. There is nothing you can do to undo what has happened. They don't call it the walk of shame for nothing, whatever the crime may be – anything that made the level of intimacy exceed the level of trust.

I created 'theological' concepts to back up why I could be a little physical (not necessarily full sexual commerce) with men, therefore justifying it nine too many times. It's only when the men became 'goners', or when I pegged it for the hills, that I really did ask, 'Why did I do that?' I swear the reason for acid reflux all those years ago was down to regretful tête-à-têtes – those moments that are not necessarily full-blown sex, but stretching the areas of grey within the boundaries of sexual interplay. Sexual endeavours that still are stretching too much intimacy for emotional safety.

Did I honour the men I slept with? Can I innocently say I treated them as kings, being happy to pass them to the next woman who might marry them? Could the men say the same about me? Maybe – maybe not. The dilemma comes when we believe an act has become the new standard, when we start to say: 'I've done that once, so what's the point in changing now?'

If you rob a bank once, does it make any difference if you rob a thousand? Seemingly so. The grace of God can't be our get-out-of-jail-free card when we are approaching that moment where we decide whether to allow seduction to help us keep the man we want to be ours for good. Will sex make him love you, or at least bring a connection? It might achieve affinity for an hour – or five. But love? Nope. And that's where the sex-slip comes in. Hope often gets mixed with the alcoholic enticement of lust and – boom – you've got your catastrophe, all reflected in the feelings of chagrin* and unhealthy soul ties. For your journals, healthy soul ties are the intertwining of two people spiritually connected in a spiritual realm. This doesn't necessarily take place without physical connection, but should this take place between two people, soul ties are often bonded with such acts. I know, it sounds so Hogwarts for anyone that's not heard this stuff before, but trust me, breaking soul ties where there is shame over someone else, is pretty crucial to your healing.

If you've done something with a man that you regret because he didn't want to marry you or commit to you, you are probably now longing for the number of Doc Brown in *Back to the Future* because you want to time travel. But you can't, because that's a fictitious film that was made up, just like the hope you created in 'sexy time'.

It's not right to ignore desires, but it is right to question what we should do next when we've acted on our desires outside of covenant.

Yes, you're right, twenty-first century, if you're protecting your genitals and being 'careful' with condoms – WHO CARES about the heart?

Shame and regret go together like a couplet, and you either share them with someone you're accountable to, someone who wants the best for you, or you can let regret kill you. If you keep it all hidden, you will begin to form a new path in your life based on those mistakes over setting the phonograph record straight, boring everyone around you with repetitive mistakes.

We're living in a society where 'normal' appears to accept having sex with anyone, as long as you've had a handshake before the boudoir. We're living in a world where liberation isn't liberation, it's just a breaking of limits. Where, apparently, moral coding shouldn't apply because gone are the days where sex was a gift from God. Yes, you're right, twenty-first century, if you're protecting your genitals and being 'careful' with condoms – WHO CARES about the heart?

The soul? Oh that ol' thing.

You know you're not a sinner right? You know that Christ is in you, yes? You have the power to condemn your own wrongdoings, and you have the power to turn on your heels and wave bye-bye to them.

Whatever is 'normal' in your everyday surroundings will exert a heavy pressure on how you perceive relationships – and everything in them. People who I worked with in the ad industry were baffled by my willingness to wait, yet I've never been more liberated than since I made this resolution. My decision-making is more rational over men, I can

I refuse to let shame get in the way of the King and I.

walk away much more easily, break-ups are far less painful and, again, my conversation with God wavers far less, because I refuse to let shame get in the way of me and my Father – the fulfiller of dreams.

If I end up physically exploring a little further than I intended to at any point, I go to God before anyone – or anything – else. I refuse to let shame get in the way of the King and I. So I reconcile. I turn back to grace. And I make changes for the next encounter with my man, because, if I haven't, then I've learnt nothing and my apology was as fake as my (Philadelphian) friend John-Paul's attempt at an English accent.

When we sense conviction – the celestial alarm system that can either ring quietly, or too loudly if we're refusing to listen – it's a time to celebrate. Yes, I said celebrate. It's not a time to run because God our Father, a Father who loves us and values who we are, is showing us something about himself. He's showing an area we've got confused in. We only mess up when we've believed a lie about ourselves, or God.

We all seem to know the Corinthians quote, 'Everything is permissible for me,' but it is not a question of your rights to free will – you have that. You can do whatever you want. But if you want to enjoy healthy relationships and you're being convicted by a feeling that is saying, 'Don't do this,' then it's God wanting to show something about himself to you. He's sending you an invitation to press in to this area. Address it. Don't pretend tomorrow is a better day. It will, without question, be filled with the same mistakes.

Those mistakes puncture us with arrows of shame so we hide away from God. I told you, any tactic to interfere between God and you is evil making pretty pathetic attempts to bulldoze you. How strong those attempts are depend on how weak you believe yourself to be.

The shame will tell you you're not good enough, it'll make you hide the importance of your slip-up, brushing it off as not a big deal. But then you'll repeat it, because you ignored the conviction, the invitation of God who was saying, 'Here's another piece of me that you can look at, I'm not sure you're understanding it, and I want to show you that I love you in your pain.' We don't believe we're holy enough to go to him and so we begin to give up. Slowly the sex-slips become nothing but a new life-style, and you start to hang out with people who will justify your 'normal'.

My 'normal' today? Well, if people have sex before marriage, or move too far into that question, 'Just how much can I get away with and still be saved?' a) you're asking the wrong question and b) it's a shock to us. Our 'normal' is holding back for marriage. Our 'normal' is also not fazed by a person's antics. So if someone is addicted to porn, or to anything that makes them believe sex is the most important thing in their universe, then the approach is not, 'You're an idiot for messing up.' Condemnation is banished from these walls and it's a case of asking questions: 'Why do you think you do it?' 'Do you feel understood – by anyone?'

Once someone has the determination to expose everything they're going through, to share it with someone they'd feel sad to disappoint but not so terrified that they couldn't approach, then breakthrough throws a party.

I've seen insane numbers come into my current church environment, learn what loving ourselves well looks like for them and seen them break off a lot of addiction, a lot of sex-slips and a lot of self-wreckage.

Just because they might have squeaky-clean purity plans, people who've never touched a naked breast may still be emotionally dysfunctional, knotted up in fear of intimacy. Know that your purity is not a direct reflection of your identity or your heart towards God like some people can make it. You only need look at King David, enticed by Bathsheba then enduring consequences much more far-reaching than he could have wished for. But God didn't leave David. Because God saw David's heart to want to put it right.

Sweet girl, ask what your normal is, ask why you're hiding when the conviction is a route for celebration – a step closer to loving yourself better. Seek no justification from an unhealthy 'normal' and step into the most loving of guidance. Having people that you can be accountable to is a vital part of this process, especially if there are addictions involved. Have people in your life that inspire you in the area you're struggling in; they are the walking vision boards of what you want to become.

Soul ties need to be broken after any form of sex-slip. Hooks sink into areas you're probably not even aware of.

The Sex-Slip

You'll know if you have soul ties – if you still think about him all the time, if you want there to be more between you two, if you want him to change his mind, if you are jealous of someone new in his life. Yes, those naughty little soul ties.

The steps to breaking out of this cycle, if left incomplete, would be like leaving a mouse inside out after a biology experiment. Finish the job by committing to a fresh approach with a renewed mind.

Then find a place, and some hours, to focus on loving yourself. Because, although conviction is vital for growth, shame will stick its heels in the mud for much longer than the lesson you've learnt. You needn't hide behind anything if you've turned 180 degrees on what happened, with an honest intention to avoid the mistake again.

When I've messed up, I can almost feel his back turn on me. He doesn't want to watch it; he can't watch me do it to myself. But he never leaves because he trusts me more than I trust myself.

Sex-slips are a reflection of what's going on in your heart and a reflection of the world you live in. There are many worlds with many different moral constructs. The one I live in today really has succeeded in loving everyone, surpassing any other community I've ever experienced. But it is still made up of humans, and they're not mistake-free.

How well I steward myself sexually is in the power of my 'no'. God watches to see how much my relationship with him matters. When I've messed up, I can almost feel his back turn on me. He doesn't want to watch it; he can't watch me do it to myself. But he never leaves because he trusts me more than I trust myself. He invented sex for the powerful connection and he can't watch if I'm misusing it for makeshift love.

Why did you do that?

That will be his first question, followed by:

Do you not love yourself the way I love you?

Can we talk about it? will always be his third.

Don't leave what we have for that, is his final say.

By then I'm undone. I'm undone to tears, to his love, to his almighty ubiquity; I'm undone as he looks at me again. And my reply *has* to be:

'May my yes always welcome your eyes and never your back. It's you who designed me. Not them.'

XX

GREAT SEXPECTATIONS

'What counts in making a happy marriage is not so much
how compatible you are but how you deal with
incompatibility.'

(Leo Tolstoy)

Since my decision to venture into a path of purity for
the last few years, the public response has been as
mixed as a United Colors of Benetton poster*. Most
respect my decision and shrug it off as if I'd told them I
had lost a packet of Wrigley's Extra chewing gum. But, for
a minority, let's just say I have to stop them from calling
Neighbourhood Watch to report a crime of Carrie abstaining from sex in the singleton years.

For the years I played it pure before, my naivety, I confess,
created some incredible methods to see how I could decipher
whether a potential future husband was going to be sexually

compatible with me. The fear had started at an early age, after all this was everyone's main argument. It didn't matter if they had addictions or the personality of a doorstop, as long as they were great in the sack. My ridiculous assessments began:

Could they dance like Patrick Swayze without over-enthusiastic shoulders? How did they handle hardware tools? Were they nifty in a game of Twister? Were they blind? (Rumour had it that lack of eyesight meant they were pretty good with all other senses. I actually sought blind men out for a time. OK, I didn't.) The questions were endless, and pointless.

You, too, may test your instincts with bizarre theories because you are terrified of the possible negative consequences if you discover on your wedding night, the first time you make love to the one man you had held out for, that you are as compatible as a mongoose and a cobra.

By now you'll know that I didn't wait until my wedding night. The experience was exactly how I thought it would be. It wasn't rocket science; if you understand your own body, then working a protractor is more complex. No one ordered fireworks, no one's head blew off. It was powerful and it was pleasant for the moment. Was it worth losing my virginity before finding the guy I will finally marry? You must be joking. The value of it, the value of the most intimate bonding between two people, fell like the NAS-DAQ index on the day of the economic crash in 2007.

Of course we hear the horror stories of people waiting till their wedding night, saving themselves with quite the purity plan, divorcing a year or two later because someone's anatomy reminded them of a 'thimble'. Or because their sex drives were completely bipolar. It's true, people do divorce, even Christians, because of sexual incompatibility.

But keep reading.

If I marry, and we've waited in our relationship for covenant, without wanting to prophetically declare this over the guy, our wedding night will probably be a three-second wonder. If he's held out for that long, I can hardly expect him to have the muscular structure of The Rock by lifting 15 lb weights for one night only. As my friends tell me, 'it is in the training'. For many, that first year of marriage is quite the laboratory of sexual exploration. But when people have genuine relationship with God above all, the two in union will want to please each other, to lay down their lives for each other – as we're meant to.

Using fear of sexual incompatibility as a reason for not waiting until marriage says to me that your God is too small. And that your love for your man is too small. Your perspective is tiny and your fear is too dominant. We only sin when we believe a lie, so be careful who you listen to.

Sexual desires shouldn't be exceeding the emotional, spiritual connection between the two of you. The areas all intertwine – if the need for sexual gratification is taking over your love for each other, then it's only a matter of time before one of you has a sore back, and the other has an affair because they believe they have the right to be given sex at any time they wish. You'll be living in fear in case you can't put out for reasons that are beyond your control.

More marriages struggle with communication (followed by disconnection and dishonesty) than sexual incompatibility.

As Anthony Hilder says: 'Sexual compatibility is only an issue if you have a self-centred view of sex, being more focused on what satisfies you and grading people as to how well they do that. If you have a selfless, giving attitude to sex, compatibility issues dissipate as sex becomes a quest to discover and please your partner – with them hopefully doing likewise. This is the key to a loving and ever-improving sex life.'[27]

More marriages struggle with communication (followed by disconnection and dishonesty) than sexual incompatibility. Sex will often stop if spouses don't have an emotional reason to be vulnerable. If there are some couples that connect on all levels but struggle in the compatibility department, then sex therapists are on hand to advise – and they do work – if you want them to.

Half the time people have no clue what they're signing up for in marriage until they have lived with each other for the first year. My parents counselled more people in their first year of marriage than at any other point. Bring kids into the equation and, oh mamma, you gotta make sex work to a whole new schedule.

Perhaps you only need to surround yourselves with honest married couples that are like my friends who, after a decade of marriage with four to five kids under their belt, will retell their wedding night as comedy material for the dinner table. You learn then that people work through stuff, the foundation to their marriage being honesty and *talking*.

The mind, body and spirit cannot be separated; you cannot cut off one from the other.

Before everyone starts throwing this book out or writes me letters telling me about how important sex is in their marriage, don't get me wrong – it's vital. Not having regular moments to physically bond will affect your mind and spirit. I am not saying that sex doesn't matter, nor that it's to be sidelined. But it mustn't be highlighted as the most important thing in marriage. It's just one of the important things.

A fundamental problem we have in the church is ignorance about sexual desires. So often we religiously shove desires under the sea grass carpet, all because of shame. Renaissance art is still hidden in crypts of some churches to hide its nude drawings of the Christ. Yet the same artworks used to be suspended on the walls of cathedrals.

It's not pretty when you see couples unable to keep each other satisfied sexually, but it's not the end of the bedroom world.

This isn't self-mortification of the flesh or seeking pain in self-denial. I'm merely saying don't be tempted to experiment for the sake of curiosity. Because marriage isn't about you, it's about both of you and if you're only after what you can get, you're missing out on the entire covenantal point. The more you see him consider your feelings, the more he can emotionally express himself without a selfish need, the more tender his heart for you, the more he'll be a loveable man, my girl.

If there's no passion in a relationship for someone you like, why would you want to be with them? There must be sexual tension in dating; it's there for you to enjoy later. Don't just sign the wedding certificate because someone had a word from the Lord or you had a prophetic dream that made you believe it was God. You must have *eros*. You must have *storge*. You must have *philia* and, for it to last, *agape* love.*

190

Great Sexpectations

Miss one of those four and you'll be back to loneliness, only this time there's someone lying right next to you each night, silently reminding you that marriage wasn't meant to be lonely.

It's not pretty when you see couples unable to keep each other satisfied sexually, but it's not the end of the bedroom world. Like most things, if they both want something to work, it will, and many do break through that hurdle, again becoming self-sacrificing to each other's desires. So often they go on to enjoy incredible new adventures with brand new insight.

If there's a man in your life that is using the possibility of incompatibility as a reason to have sex with you before marriage, send him a greeting basket and skip to your heart's content. This can't be reckoned with manipulation, ultimatums or fear. If he really can't do a relationship without sex before marriage, then he's being honest – so respect that and let him go.

This isn't the eighties any more, where money's for nothing, nor are the chicks free, so bye-bye Dire Straits, let this be a new age where hearts cost something, the chicks aren't cheap and compatibility starts soul- not skin-deep.

CARRIE'S PRACTICAL POINTERS

- **Remember, you're not avoiding sex because you hate post-modernism as much as the National Trust.** You're not out of date; you're bang on form for a royal, heavenly government who values you more than much of today's society. I've never seen people hurt others by saving themselves for marriage; it's usually the opposite. Sexuality is normal; desires are part of our wiring. Avoid prudishness on this subject.

- You needn't succumb to FOMO, or the fear of rejection. No person who values themself feels pressure to be like others. **Keep close friendships with those who hold the same values as you do on lifestyle.** Enjoy your individuality, still choose your instinctive heart over popularity.

- **Sexual intimacy is intended to be gorgeous, to be powerful – so value it, by valuing you.** Sex wasn't intended to be all animal and no love. If it were, it wouldn't be so powerful. There is fun in the forbidden, but fun can also be found in honour, joyful connection and selflessness. We can't compartmentalize the Bible; if you're justifying your faith and purity mishaps by twenty-first-century concepts, you'll miss out on relationships that could blow your beautiful mind.

- **Desires are healthy, it's how you're made.** The desires themselves are not sinful, it's what you do with them. Are you hurting others? Are you subconsciously using others? Are you willing to commit sincerely or are you still not sure? Don't light the match, if you're not certain you want to burn with them.

- **Set some limits between you and your man.** I know what my triggers are (alpha males, high dominant personalities, wine-filled late nights). People have different 'purity plans'. Talk through physical boundaries often. **Be careful to not go back and forth on your parameters, as it will eat away trust.**

- **Don't let shame destroy intimacy.** Face the mistake, see conviction as an invitation to know something new about how papa God sees you, but don't hide from the boyfriend – or God. That would hurt both hearts. This is where the secret place is put to the test. Make it a point not to regress, or hold onto something you've already processed.

- **Porn does harm others** – not only for the ethical reasons of sex trafficking and the industry, but it entices your brain to need more shock value – therefore building a need for animal desires from others. Coming off porn can be difficult to do alone. Find someone to process this with. There are hundreds of organizations you can talk to. It's not embarrassing; it's just your natural desire that got aligned to the wrong path, which won't bring you the best sex life or the closest intimacy that you deserve.

- **Can the success of a relationship be determined by sexual compatibility?** If this is the question being asked, I suggest shadowing a marriage counselling session to see what really is needed in longevity. You *must* find your guy sexually attractive in dating, but this can't be the decisive factor. If it is the excuse for giving everything of you before marriage, there will be other areas where you'll be conditional with your love as well.

PART V

HEARTBREAK MOTEL

Break-ups can be the art of your healing or the death of it. Scars could occur instead of repairable wounds, but of course you cannot control what others may do, you can only control your reactions. There are some key motivations that need to be confronted in this section: the art of the break-up in the first place, forgiveness, banishing shame and retreating from the intrigue of following up old flames. I've been lucky enough to have dated some great men who have shown such respect in a separation (no gossip, no justification, apologies, humility, no scorecards) that we've remained friends afterwards and it is these experiences that I am thankful for, for it is here that you realized they truly loved you.

XXI

MOLESKINE AND MINK

'He heals the broken-hearted and binds up their wounds.'
(Psalm 147:3)

There's no denying it: break-ups monumentally blow. There's the nausea, the swollen eye sockets, the 'What would Bridget Jones do?' and the three billion questions going through your mind, all ending in – 'why?'

There may be very obvious reasons why you parted ways, but the fact remains, you have, and Toni Braxton's 'Un-break My Heart' blurting out at 10,000 decibels will not help. A little reflection in the Word, kindness to yourself and some cookie dough ice cream might ease things. Dairy intolerant? Then you're in for a rough ride.

The first time I recognized that I handled mourning rather poorly was when my mother found me digging up my dwarf lop rabbit, which we had buried two weeks before. So bereft was I over losing Rambo (don't ask), that I didn't want to accept that he was gone. In years to come my handling of heartbreaks wasn't much better. Especially when it came to denial of it being over – clutching at straws and attempts at reigniting love were often embarrassing. Let me give you an example:

'Oh hey, hey Simon, hey. I wondered if you had my Nirvana album? I can't seem to find it.'

'No. I don't.'

'You don't what?'

'I don't have it.'

Cue hysterical laughter to show how well I'm handling the break-up: 'OH! HAHA HAH AHA.'

Silence.

'So how are you? Is everything OK? Are you perfect? Are you ugly yet?'

'I'm good. Just about to go out with my mum.'

'YOU'RE GOING OUT WITH WHO?!'

'Goodbye Carrie.'

He hangs up.

The older I got the more I realized manipulation to seek revenge or win them back was as disastrous as Heather Mills discussing her divorce with Paul McCartney on the TV breakfast show *Daybreak*.* That moment where she went ultrasonic in voice tone started a symphony of dogs barking in gardens, perturbing quite a large chunk of Britain, while other more compassionate folk tilted their heads

198

to one side saying, 'Oh bless her. It'll take half the time they were together to recover.'

Unfortunately, these days social networking has catapulted broken hearts into a whole world of crazy. Write a deranged status update and it could go viral:

'I know I screwed up badly. I know that I hurt you. Going to jail changed me greatly. I love you – just know that, even if I never hear from you again.'

A comment underneath read: 'Maybe text her this mate?'

With the response: 'I can't – court orders.'

Please don't do the subliminal messaging/post up photos of random cute boys/stalk him thing. Just don't. You can only be responsible for your actions, not his. The quicker you accept the pain of this, facing it head on, the quicker you heal. But face it you must. Otherwise you might start calling him in the middle of the night because you can't remember how to make his special Marmite on toast recipe. It's a knife full of Marmite, spread on toast. And you're not fooling anyone.

If he shows no remorse or feeling in the conversation, then, my sweet stranger, you're so much better out of the relationship.

Seek closure above all. In *that* conversation with him, whoever is wishing to pull away, ask questions rather than making assumptions. Let your heart be known by sharing how you feel, ensuring you've processed this many times before you actually speak to him to avoid emotionally charged conversations or passive aggression; in traumatic times like this, you don't want to do anything you will regret in five minutes, never mind in one year.

It's easier for your healing process if he does give you reasons (if he ends the relationship), but if he's unable to give you any, then realize that you've been freed from a man who can't get in touch with his heart at all. If he shows no remorse or feeling in the conversation, then, my sweet stranger, you're so much better out of the relationship. If you end it, make sure you give him feedback that he can either take and learn from or simply shut down – that's up to him. Own what you must and leave the rest.

Once *the conversation* has been as witty as Ricky Gervais, as emotional as that final scene in *Gone with the Wind* and as intellectual in reflection as *Question Time** (one can dream), then it is time to purge. Get the pain out. Get it out like you would food poisoning. Don't resist; just let your organs, your emotions, your soul do what it needs to do to break all ties.

But how do you break away well?

Well, if he couldn't help you make parting amicable (he got antagonistic/defensive), create your own closure by writing down your core values. Write down the deterrents learnt. Take ownership rather than pointing the blame or writing bitter IOU spreadsheets to him. No rebounds. You'll only be with the same type again.

This takes guts but it's possible. Very possible – if you like yourself. Develop a muscle memory that doesn't involve him in it. Make time every day to cry, shout, wallow in the happy and hurtful times. Not in the town square, but in the privacy of your own home. This is important. Not processing the pain will mean you leave no room to find compassion for the other person. Rinse the feelings out by confronting them again and again until you begin to feel them change. So, when you are alone, grasp the pain by the horns and become the matador to the emotions until they die.

Get a Moleskine journal (the paper is more durable for such tears) and write it all down. For God is recording every thought you have: 'You've kept track of my every toss and turn through the sleepless nights, each tear entered in your ledger, each ache written in your book' (Psalm 56:8, *The Message*).

Most importantly, ask God for the truths about the lies you've been hearing. God may comfort you, but he may also bring you the things you need to know in order to move forward, even if the process is incredibly painful. Remember, he is your Father and longs for the best for you. Sometimes that means teaching you through the pain.

In a break-up not too many moons ago, I wasn't protected from my ex's commentary to mutual friends and it was just the tonic I needed in order to move on. When attempts to sabotage and not protect your character are made through the power of words, it's a clear tale that they are feeling a need for revenge, for self-justification for poor behaviour – or they never had a core value to honour you. It's easy to walk away at that point. There's nothing inviting to stay for. But still, forgive them we must so we can trust our next partner and love him utterly.

> **When I see people vent on everyone it screams of an insecurity within, a desire for others to fix or justify it, rather than face the reality of the pain.**

Reach out to mentors, your spiritual fathers and mothers, and involve them in the healing process. Have an ear that not only listens, but also applies the wisdom. Seek people who aren't interested in bashing the ex, but are more eager to build you up. There is a difference. If they bash the man you chose to show a little of your heart to, their slamming of his imperfections won't bring revelation to you – only a short-term fix to a deeper problem.

In addition, make sure you don't go to everyone to talk about your break-up. Pick your council of advisors wisely, as seeking a hundred bits of advice will distract you from your healing process and your conversations with God. When I see people vent on everyone it screams of an insecurity within, a desire for others to fix or justify it, rather than face the reality of the pain. It's unlikely the person is talking to God or seeking comfort in him.

My finest and healthiest break-up was probably with my boyfriend of five years. We had lived with each other (another tale), worked with each other, loved each other through thick and thin. But we got to that deciding moment where we knew we couldn't marry due to very different core values – it wouldn't be fair on future children.

We sat down and for hours would discuss how to break apart. We took our time, considering each other's feelings and reaching out to say how much it was sucking. We levied everything from being friends on social media (disconnecting until we'd healed) right through to furniture, financial business accounts and the dog. We sat Nicodemus, my Pomeranian, who was chosen by my boyfriend when he was a six-week-old puppy, on the bed:

'Mummy and Daddy are going to divorce,' we told him. His head turned at 180-degree angles. 'But we want you to know we love you very much and will look after you all your life. In fact you'll probably get twice as many presents.' Both of us were crying and laughing all at the same time. It was a bittersweet healing because we gave nobody a chance to share unsolicited advice with either of us in our very intimate relationship. It ensured the process was nothing but a pleasant reflection.

I've never regretted that relationship because the break-up was handled with chivalry. Most of the healing is in the actual moment of break-up and if the man has been controlling, unsafe and you've had to pull away quickly, it can be harder to recover, but you can, with the help of wise friends and spiritual brothers who remind you that not all men play this way.

The subsequent few months were painful and teary, and because my feelings for him were so genuine I couldn't look at another man for nine months. I would make vision boards of what I wanted for the future year. The saddest part was that I couldn't involve one of the finest men I had ever known.

I asked God to give me hope in what seemed to be a bleak future; what followed in the year ahead was an entire move to California, new men whom I could connect with and a whole other level of healthy relationships. I followed up with emails to the ex, apologizing for the times I got it wrong. Of course he had forgiven me before I had even sent any emails. Such is the beauty of people who respect each other over and above what they can get out of it themselves.

Embrace it as a time for understanding a new part of God you've never discovered before.

Be warned: you may have the occasional ex-boyfriend who is so uncomfortable in himself when bumping into you, he will take those 180 seconds to say how he's not drinking because he's lifting weights, yet has been *so* drunk in the Lord recently. To which you should smile politely, confirming how 'happy' you are for him, sighing with relief that he is no longer the guy you need to be responsible to. Think 'phew', not 'ouch'.

Don't use such moments to prove something to yourself or to them. Remember, your value is in God, not any boyfriend. When the emotions are realistic, it's so much easier when you bump into them and they acknowledge you once meant something to each other.

Breaking up takes time – there is no quick fix. Embrace it as a time for understanding a new part of God you've never discovered before. Reflect on you and what made you attracted to the guy in the first place – and what were the elements that didn't make it longer term?

In amongst the heartache, go have fun. Find your girls, wear faux mink, pearls and your killer heels. Find all those things that make you love being a woman. And remind yourself of all those things that God loves about you.

The boyfriend didn't define you, God did – and still does. The boy's love for you may have hit the rejected pile, but your destiny is still unfinished and you have a job to do. For now, that starts with picking yourself up and finding forgiveness for him – so that bitterness doesn't hold you back from falling in love again. Forgiveness will not enter the building until your soul has had a clear-out of anger, bitterness, pain and confusion.

You are loved by an entity far more impressive than the enlightening tastes you had from the relationship. So sink into the Father until it's safe to come out and rest in the knowledge that everyone deserves unconditional love. Seek wisdom and kindness, time for your heart and God's, rebound only in healthy activities and seek today a strength that will make you bolder than brass for tomorrow.

Remember, you were made for the world, not for the boyfriend. So this, too, shall pass.

XXII

POISON IN A PINT

'Shame corrodes the very part of us that believes we are
capable of change.'
(Brené Brown, *I Thought It Was Just Me: Women
Reclaiming Power and Courage in a Culture of Shame*)

It is the most terrifying moment when you decide to accept yourself completely. Or so I've heard. Most of the time, we all carry a little hip flask of shame, a soupçon of self-condemnation that seeks a top-up whenever we get a startling reminder of a mistake we've made, or a wrongdoing we've caused. Sometimes it's a wrongdoing to ourselves that we never want anyone to know about. Sometimes we carry shame because we don't risk at all.

We have apologized. We have said our Hail Marys. We have sat in a confessional box for 300 hours as if it were community service. We have written letters to our victims

207

and to ourselves. We have gone over the reasons why we did what we did. We have heard audible voices from the Lord. We have even watched Mel Gibson's *The Passion of the Christ* just to have one more reminder that Christ died for us.

Somehow, lugging around shame is what we believe we should do. We wouldn't want anyone to think that we believed our actions were justified.

But, somehow, lugging around shame is what we believe we should do. We wouldn't want anyone to think that we believed our actions were justified. I've seen married men, after intense extra-marital affairs, carry webcams on their person so their wives know where they are at all times. For the record, it wasn't her idea. It was his.

People push fear to the back burner, thinking they've moved on. I've come to believe that muffling emotions is what turns subconscious feelings into poisonous self-medication, harsh condemnation towards others or a repetition of the same crime. Sex addicts often don't do it *for* the thrill, they do it *from* the shame.

In April 2013, I flew to the Philippines to counsel eleven rescued victims of sex trafficking. An interpreter, a colleague and I sat down with one 17-year-old, let's call her Clementine, who had been rescued from 'the bars' – known as brothels to you and me.

She couldn't look me in the eyes. Maybe because she knew divulging her stories meant I was about to stare evil in the face. What she didn't know was that I wasn't afraid to spit right into its dirty, emaciated eyeballs.

'Are you ready?' I asked my interpreter.

'As ready as we'll ever be,' she breathed deeply.

I looked to my teammate and told her to chip in at any point. We managed well on facial expressions and sign language throughout the hour. So we began attempting eye contact, as I spoke:

'I need you to know a few things. Anything you tell me is received without judgement, and in confidentiality as long as you aren't in current danger. If you are, I will need to tell those who look after you. We want to know your story and how you think we can help you. Is that OK?'

She nodded, paused, then began to speak: 'Alright, here it is. I was selling my body until four weeks ago.'

She was taking ownership, she wasn't playing victim, despite the sexual abuse she had suffered from her family and the manipulation she had faced in the brothels. She was feisty. And I liked it.

I wish I had lined my stomach beforehand, though, as I began to hear the detail of her story. Molestation and rape from brothers, father, uncles. Her mother fell ill, which ended in her living in hospital. Her father left. She had no education, no income, not enough food to feed her siblings.

209

So she grabbed a job at a bar through the introduction of one of her friends.

She began by waitressing and developed a reputation for working at one of those 'bars', so was soon labelled a prostitute. Rejected by her mother as a result, and with no education, she had no choice other than to provide an 'extra service' in the bar – from the age of 15. As she told her story, my head began to swell and my imagination got the better of me. I began to see visions of us advisors holding imaginary AK47s pointing towards the line-up of evil stories coming in our path.

So this is what going from glory to glory looks like? No warning came to tell me it looked this ugly. Her tears fell all over the place, on her jeans, on my dress and right into my own soul.

Forget *Days of Our Lives.* You want drama? It's right here. And it's full of agony, disease and incest.

First impressions from my personal tale to hers would tell you we were worlds apart in our perspectives. But in the corners of our minds, we shared the same need. To fly in freedom.

'Shall I tell you what freedom looks like?' I whispered. She looked into my eyes for the first time. 'It looks like unchaining yourself from the unforgiveness you have towards the torture you've suffered. No more do you stay suffering in shame. It's time to get this pain out. I'm giving you a journal so you can write it all down. No names, no locations, in case you lose it. Then burn it.

'Then you need to know your worth on this planet. I need you to understand that what these people have done to you is not acceptable, it is evil, it is dumbfounding – and they are broken. Only you can decide you can be powerful, strong, a fighter for your own freedom and a force for good. You need to start forgiving these people – and yourself. You needn't ever see them again, but we need to help you leave the baggage behind. Otherwise you'll stay in unhealthy relationships, believe you deserve abuse and you'll judge everyone – including yourself. You'll live in constant fear and hatred. And you're better than that. I know it.'

I looked at her face and on her right cheek she had a beauty spot. This rocked me, because I had had a dream about a girl with a beauty spot on her right cheek two months before my trip. I'd been asking God to highlight people to me for this time in the Philippines. No wonder my soul felt so warm towards her.

I put the pen down.

'I've just been reminded of something,' I said to the interpreter. 'I'm about to change the scheme of things here.'

'OK?'

'Tell her I was given a dream about her two months ago.' She began to interpret my words. I saw Clementine's face begin to change. Written all over it was, 'You mean I was in a plan? Before I even stopped selling my body?'

I carried on: 'From all the things you have endured, all the things you faced, you will rescue a hundred times more girls than I ever could. You are meant to build bridges for hope and rescue the dying souls of the Philippines. The rebellion you showed at times against your family – that made you fight for your name – will continue but this time it will be for freedom. You're a fighter, defiant to the end. You will not give up. You know the darkest side of man, and you can overcome it by saving many more like you. Do you understand how special you are to have been shown to me? God has anointed you with an inner willpower that will not stumble, that will not be left on the floor.'

Shame is as poisonous as cyanide. It cuts off intimacy and brings fear in a 360-degree radius.

The Philippines is a country built on shame culture; in no other place on earth is it harder to escape it. But Clementine managed to. In a matter of days she had made a decision to go back to school, and to become a freedom fighter. I think about her all the time because, before she was the age I lost my virginity, she had already overcome shame that could have been a resident in her soul forever. Instead she faced the pain and achieved something that few manage to in their entire lives.

Shame is as poisonous as cyanide. It cuts off intimacy and brings fear in a 360-degree radius. By consciously declaring that God's love can disinfect shame, we begin to walk with our heads held upright. If we have turned about and changed our ways, then we've grown from the lesson and we are willing to walk again. But carrying shame only reminds us of an old skin we should have shed long before.

If a prostitute who endured such terrible torture can slowly brush off degradation and bathe herself in the forgiveness of God then we, too, can eradicate the remnants of opprobrium. You *can* learn to love again – this time, to the full.

XXIII

THESE HEELS WEREN'T MADE FOR REVERSING

'Do two people walk hand in hand if they aren't going to
the same place?'

(Amos 3:3, *The Message*)

There are some things that you just don't do. Most of us would agree that voting for the UK Independence Party, reading the *Daily Mirror* or dousing someone in petrol, are things we, perhaps, shouldn't do.

Here's what else we shouldn't do. Go back to the ex.

Did she just put dousing someone in petroleum on the same par as going back to the ex-boyfriend? Yes – I did. You/he self-sabotaged, had no boundaries, had no desire to compromise or compromised too much, kept going to your caves without explaining it to each other and he had the personality of a bullfrog. Yet you want him back?

You've tried to make it work. Different methods, different wardrobes, different ground rules. But the self-help books never seem to do the trick. Your intrinsic core values concord as well as Ghandi reading Madonna's 1992 book, *Sex*.

But you're planning to return because he can play the guitar? So can Gene Simmons. Because he's a nice guy? So is Ronnie Corbett. He's the hottest man you made out with? Sweetheart, you haven't travelled enough.

I dare not claim to know everything about relationships, but this is an area that I'm happy to guide you through blindfolded. I learnt a great deal through the pain of trying to manipulate my way to win the boys back, through the cunning use of the LBD* and heels so killer I had nosebleeds from the high altitude. So let my pain, be your gain.

Years ago, I didn't live with much hope of finding a future man suitable for me. I just settled. I didn't look at the long-term game plan before I fell into the murky waters. I gave emotional attachments right of reign and before you could say Bob's your pyscho-boyfriend, I didn't know whose soul was whose. Despite the fact that many of our ethics were as aligned as Goofy's orthodontic treatment, I wanted to believe my fight could turn things around and make the relationship work. If I forgave that, or I worked harder on this. I didn't take ownership of my emotions or my reactions to what I was given. That type of fight is for marriage. Right now, you're fighting for the right fit.

Thanks to my LBD-premeditated plans, I'd go back and I'd be happy in his arms. For two weeks.

You see, no matter how often you try to fill the cracks with joint compound, the cracks are still there and the foundation to the relationship is as stable as subsidence.

Why do we insist on trying to make wrong relationships work?

So why do we insist on trying to make wrong relationships work?

It's not the fear of being alone. (Loneliness is more palpable when you're in the wrong relationship.) No, the u-turning will continue for as long as hopelessness stays sheltered in your mind.

Threatening to leave doesn't change them. They are who they are, unless they decide to change themselves. If you believe your actions can change their heart, then quit manipulating and ask why you are trying to control the one you supposedly love?

So, what is it that keeps us there?

Guilt, shame, self-questioning, irrationality of age, what others think, what the family thinks, what culture expects of us, pressure we place on ourselves, self-doubt over how we behaved, insecurity, a need to be loved, co-dependency, a need to fix others, a need to fix ourselves, a fear of the unknown, a fear of stretching outside, a fear of discovering how different we are when alone, a fear of rejection, a fear of compromise, a fear of selfishness, a fear of having no one to hide behind, are just a 'couple' of the reasons that immediately come to mind – the underlying factoid being – they are all lies.

Why do great women, who believe in a heaven that has enough power to line the pavements with platinum, settle for walking on cement sidewalks in their relationships?

Above all, you just won't have peace if you stay in the relationship, and that will niggle. That voice will never shut up. Your heart deserves a megaphone, not asphyxiation. Turn off the brain and ask how your heart really feels. Then honour the answer and stick to it. Your heart is not the addict. Your brain is. Your brain holds the neurological pathways to become addicted to emotions, but we can believe it's what our hearts desire. It's why declarations are often so powerful, as the spoken word of positive thinking will begin to challenge the brain from negative self-talk. There is a reason why pastors such as Steve Backland make their entire ministry focused on the power of declarations. So learn to know the difference.

Why do great women, who believe in a heaven that has enough power to line the pavements with platinum, settle for walking on cement sidewalks in their relationships?

We're royalty, so, if we really believe that, we are whole and should have standards derived from worth not neediness.

Until we really enjoy the uniqueness of ourselves, and learn to love it, we'll be happy to accept anyone who will take us. No? And we'll continue to deprive ourselves what we actually deserve, turning off the opportunities – even our own eyes – to the right teammates for us.

Use your killer heels to keep moving *forward*, because at some point the belief in yourself, the values you have and the hope you cling on to, will bring you to places you never dreamt of, towards friendships and adventures that rouse your world.

As Isaiah 43 says, 'Remember not the former things, nor consider the things of old. Behold, I am doing a new thing; now it springs forth, do you not perceive it? I will make a way in the wilderness and rivers in the desert' (Isaiah 43:18–19, ESV).

You heal (just as mentioned in chapter XXI). You move on and, before you know it, you're sharing thoughts about current relationship adventures and sending your love to his current partner.

As a woman who now uses stilettos for pleasure, instead of using them as a relationship soldering iron, nothing, and I mean nothing, compares to the power of walking forward. By honouring ourselves, profound decisions are created that, in turn, will always venerate the heart – not expunge it.

It's time to make life decisions rooted in love. Not nostalgic need.

XXIV

THE F WORD

'Without forgiveness, there's no future.'

(Desmond Tutu)

Forgiveness is similar to judo. It is an art form that must be motivated with a fighting spirit, with no choice but to hold on throughout the battle until you've won. Forgiveness fights against the opponents of unforgiveness and bitterness, throwing them down to the mat to achieve victory. At the same time, we fight against ourselves – how to react to the heinous thoughts and crimes of others that hurt us. And yet we must learn to react using the same approach as Judo, which means: 'the gentle way'.

Absolution cannot be given by retaliating for, as my late Grandma James would tell you, 'revenge has two graves'. Yet our minds create a wild imagination of the justice we could seek within the confusion of our hurt. We want everyone to join in on our pain, backing up how gruesome the other person's soul is to cheat, lie, steal, kill and dishonour. Character defamation has never been so tempting, along with those angry subliminal social online statuses. But their ugliness begins to cultivate our own beastly disfiguration. Our souls are not what they were before the event, barely being able to recognize our own eyes in mirrors.

Years can pass by, with us still carrying this hardened shell filled with acridity, not even noticing the change in ourselves. For the emotion of bitterness has become our guarded friend, ensuring we never get vulnerable – so no one can hurt us again.

I know what you're thinking: this person sounds like a royal champion. What a true skip in the park they are. Maybe this is who you are right now, and you've not noticed.

This is the greatest misconception in Christianity, which has given us our PR image of Scrooge rather than Saint Nicholas. Communities divide, intimacy suffocates amongst the church family and, before you know it, no one is allowed to make a mistake – whether you're the canon of St Paul's Cathedral or the caretaker of the tiny Easton-On-The-Hill's parish. Because congregations never fully knew how to forgive. Oh they all say they have forgiven each other, but you only need to see their interaction with a past loved one to know they've not forgiven them any more than Scar forgave Mufasa in *The Lion King*. They still harbour feelings of antipathy, although outwardly 'they've forgiven'. Of course they have – because the Bible tells them to.

Hearts as gelid as frosted snow form in the very people who once loved others beautifully. If only they'd drop the grudge. Soon nobody will remember the hurt that caused the bitterness, for it was years since their mother abused them, or their father left them, yet we can't ignore the hurt silently screaming from the person whose whole life has been constructed to avoid hurt or pain. It so often, ironically, results in self-sabotage, with them wandering around like an island.

You want to know why some men and women don't follow through with falling in love? Just ask how their relationship is with their mother or father. Fearful of gauging emotions that place them on a vulnerable platform, it's much easier to list a few things wrong with each (wo)man they initially liked, than face the real demon within – the resentment of their own parent(s). It's one of a few reasons to explain their lack of care when they drop people from a great height. It's a constant hopscotch of living in reaction to pasts that should have been shown grace a long time ago.

It's so easy to forgive someone who has hurt you when they're kneeling at your front door with snot-infested tears running down the guitar they're serenading you on, begging for an acknowledgement that they didn't really mean it. It's so much harder to forgive when they laugh in the face of your adversity. Or, worse yet, when they just run to the attentive arms of another within days.

However, forgiveness is really a self-repair programme that is required in order for you to love yourself – and to love others without fear. Forgiveness is the way to avoid depression, low self-esteem and the toxin caused by acerbity. This isn't fluff, this is basic biology.

> **Forgiveness is the way to avoid depression, low self-esteem and the toxin caused by acerbity. This isn't fluff, this is basic biology.**

The alternative to forgiveness – living with bitterness and resentment – is like injecting yourself with strychnine yet expecting the enemy to die.

I wouldn't dream of suggesting that cancer is caused by bitterness. However, I've seen people go forward for prayer for healing in Bethel Church in California, and there have been times when specific prophetic words were spoken in those prayers that highlighted a person or a situation that the person wanting prayer needed to forgive. So often they acknowledged, for example, that they've not spoken to their father for eighteen years and it's caused huge pain. In some cases, as they've made a decision to forgive that person for their own sake, for their own peace, tumours have been known to burst in front of our eyes. Medical reports then back up later that the cancer, confusingly for the doctors, has gone.

So let's not take for granted those niggling thoughts, that unhealthy relationship with a parent, that hurt caused by the friend who seemed perfectly fine while you cried into the floorboards.

'But there are just some things you can't forgive,' is the classic go-to response that I hear echo the rooms of counselling sessions and coffee shops.

Forgiveness is not the notion that you open the cell door the moment a prisoner has whispered 'sorry'. It does not condone the most heinous of crimes. It doesn't condone at all. It does not mean we are ignoring the hurt it's caused.

This isn't a tactic to benefit the person we're forgiving, but to benefit ourselves. Just like ice can't stay the same in sub-Saharan temperatures, I do believe that unforgiveness cannot survive when you truly love yourself.

When I really love who I am on the best of my days, I find it incredibly hard to harbour ill feelings towards those who have hurt me. It is easy to jab pride in the collar bone and humble myself because I know that I, too, have hurt others. I know that I didn't deserve their treatment, but I'm strong enough to know that their hurt was not about me personally, but about their own brokenness.

So how do we forgive? A dose of getting out the anger, a spoonful of sharing the mess in the secret place, a punch or two of a pillow and finally a grasping of their life to

223

attempt to understand (not condone) the brokenness that led them to hurting you.

It is only here that forgiveness begins. Do not, I repeat, do not ignore the importance of rinsing and squeezing out the flannel of hardship, else you'll not be able to begin to absorb love from God. You'll just build up another wall that no one will be able to see you through.

Walking through pain is the only way to forgiveness. We *have* to face it – so if you didn't, go back and work through Chapter XXI again. We need to work through the torment to come through the other side, all the while being gentle on ourselves but as messy as we want to be in front of our Father. Some of my favourite moments are when I bring my whole self back together in the only place I am never truly judged but, rather, fully accepted. It is from there that in public I can rationally respond to someone whose thoughtlessness could have broken me for more than a day. It is from there that I can smile at them and shake them by the hand. It is from there that I can form a new boundary, knowing perhaps that we have very different core values.

I've had seasons in which I've struggled to forgive, but the joy I've found in my faith is the realization that I can turn to the very God who forgave me before I was even imagined in his mind. I've got Christ who exampled it, and I can love them from afar if I deem them unsafe to play with. You ask me how do we forgive? Not with a pseudo forgiveness, but with a forgiveness that lines the very wall of our gut. As I sat in the car one evening musing over those who've got a track record for reconciling the best, I asked John-Paul for his thoughts on forgiveness:

'It's so simple actually. Pops, who are they? What are they? Who were they originally? Give me the original blueprints. You look at original blueprints. You see their architecture of who they are, and how they line up. You can't

This process is impossible as long as there is pride, fear of emotion or an unwillingness to become vulnerable. For only emotional leverage will make you change perspective.

help but be impressed. You can't be genuinely impressed by someone and still have unforgiveness towards them. I don't mean "wow he's impressive". I mean the Lord has in-pressed that person upon you. When you see them like that, anybody that's a human that has a heart, that's pumping blood, that's hot. You can't help but change.'[28]

Most people of faith understand the theological dictum behind the need for forgiveness. Christ didn't suffer the world's most intolerable capital punishment just for you to scupper the thesis, poisoning yourself with hatred towards someone who stole your Nokia twelve years ago. Or even towards the one who trafficked your body, like the girls I've counselled. Most righteous believers know *why* they should forgive, but they are still faced with palpitations, defensive reactions and distrust towards people after they've suffered one of the three Ds: divorce, death or disarming of the soul.

When you've worked through the pain, the compassion comes a little easier and you become fed up of being fed up. This process is impossible as long as there is pride, fear of emotion or an unwillingness to become vulnerable. For only emotional leverage will make you change perspective.

Ten years ago, I walked into an art exhibition purely by accident. It showed a bunch of photographs of unrecognizable faces. The visuals were about as entertaining as my own cooking (that's not a good thing) but the stories attached to them changed my mind.

From Desmond Tutu to a mother who had lost her son after a drunk driver killed him, all stories were based on their journey to forgiveness. Genuine 'heart-meant' forgiveness.

In another story, two married missionaries had been taken hostage by Chechnyan soldiers, for fourteen torturous months. The wife was taken into another room and repeatedly raped by one of the guards, while the husband was handcuffed to heated pipes. It's a scene that doesn't happen to many of us and, as she contracted herpes, terrified of raising an alarm in case the other soldiers developed the idea of gang rape, the couple faced more pain than most could survive. Within her mind, the wife refused to let the rapist damage her inner peace, knowing her body was not all of her.

The husband repeatedly fantasized about murdering the soldier but instead chose to react with prayer for the solider. On release, despite the joy and the freedom from captivity, the wife collapsed and they both needed some time to be apart to heal, recover and go through their own emotional recovery.

Once they both admitted the pain, through weakness and vulnerability, they were slowly able to heal, acknowledging the guards were bred from bad behaviour. There was an understanding, but not atonement. They weren't planning to reconcile with their captors, but still they found freedom in the F word.

Nobody wins when they've found revenge. I've never seen vendettas mend anyone's soul, just break it more. I've never seen love come from those who don't believe in forgiveness. Restoration does occur in those who believe that God seeks justice, but have accepted that it may not happen on their watch.

My words might just be black and white formations, which seem too distant to grasp. You may have a fear of letting go, perhaps, in case you are considered weak. But there is freedom in this viewpoint that evokes a supreme strength. Maybe you just need inspiration, so how about:

Yvonne Stern, who in 2010 forgave her husband's affair along with the mistress who hired a hit man to kill her in three separate attempts. Or the dismantlement of the Berlin Wall in 1989. What about Mandela's pardon, which affected the apartheid of South Africa. Or Gordon Wilson's forgiveness towards the IRA bombers who killed his daughter, rocking the peace movement for Northern Ireland. Or even Ruby Bridges who, in 1960, aged 6, prayed along the corridors of an all-white school in New Orleans while others shouted, threw things and threatened poisoning. She set the course for the beginning of integrated schools.

Your power is not in the withholding of mercy; your power only comes to fruition in your pardon.

Never underestimate the power of the pardon. People only ever remember the names of those who refused to hide behind the pain and forgave those who caused the atrocities they suffered. No one remembers the names of other relatives of the IRA victims, just Gordon Wilson – because that's how grace startles souls.

The freedom of forgiveness creates a domino effect of love, which has, in some cases, changed the course of history forever.

Your power is not in the withholding of mercy; your power only comes to fruition in your pardon. Isn't it time to begin to face the grudges that hold little resemblance to your current pain? For within the amnesty of the process, you will see your own reflection in all its clarity and in all its beauty.

The F Word

Let no one hold the very peace you were given from the beginning of time any more. Be courageous, and learn to understand that impunity was never a battle of the egos, nor a battle of the scorecard.

The goal of forgiveness was always to love you and therefore God first.

CARRIE'S PRACTICAL POINTERS

- Heartache? Get it out. Get it out. Get it out. **It's quicker to heal when you confront.** Write, shout it out and talk to a select few who can keep your entire process in absolute confidence, especially within a community such as church. Steer clear of sharing anything with mutual friends. If they ask questions, then answer, but avoid detail, no matter how much he might have hurt you.
- **Whatever you focus on will get bigger.** In a break-up, the key is to keep eyes on your own heart, not the boyfriend's actions. Apologize where you need to. Resolve. If he is creating defence or not taking some ownership, this will be more difficult. Learn to accept unresolved conflict by keeping your identity sited in God's opinion of you. If the ex doesn't respond to your request for respect (that's a clear sign he needs to do some work of his own) rest in your mentors, friends, retro-roller-skating and the secret place.
- **The healing is often in the break-up itself.** If he honours you, he should give some time and space before

telling everyone. It's wise for you both to face the pain without an immediate public announcement. He needs to protect you by not using a slandering tongue. If he is not covering you (gossiping, inaccurate stories, character defamation), create strong boundaries and ask him to stop. Friends who care for you or justice will also confront him on any slander or 'pity-pulling'.

- **Scorecards aren't from heaven.** Avoid distracting yourself by holding scorecards or revenge tactics. Maybe he owes you something – let it go, or you will appear begrudging, only loving him for 'things' or money or the relationship.

- **Guard your heart from friends who take sides, or gossip.** This is where you use discernment and decide who to rely on most. Mature men will not need affirmation from your friends or the community; they will not hope people take sides. If people have cut you off, they've helped you in realizing who your real friends are. **Kingdom people will love you regardless of any break-up, any mistake you made, or any mistake he made.**

- My exes usually bless the new man in my life – that's Kingdom, that's honour, that's *healthy*. **You want to be able to bless each other in new relationships.** Because people are not your property until marriage.

- **The poison of shame is often hidden behind extreme judgement, blame, self-sabotage, pride or inability to be able to take criticism.** Is the past left behind? Go

231

to God for the truth and tell him you're sorry, or if it's someone else's actions against you, have a brother/father figure apologize to you on their behalf.

- Forgiveness takes time, so accept that the pain will be there for a bit. **Be intentional about forgiving, for the sake of your own healing.** As you keep processing the feelings in the secret place, by writing or in therapy if serious cases of sexual abuse, emotional abuse, etc. have occurred. As you begin to change your outlook, you'll invite more compassion in.

- It's going to be OK, because every tear is recorded, and nothing goes unnoticed. Remember that there is someone fighting to get you your dreams and **he will not stop – even when you've had enough.**

PART VI

THE THREE STOOGES

The three stooges are three perspectives that I've seen hold back many great women from healthy relationships and joy-led lives: the victim mentality, the fear of being single and the belief that there are no more men out there worthy to be loved. Years of experiences, years of grafting have taken their toll on some women, and I'm trusting these few chapters will be the final stage to get you tiptoeing and beatboxing to your hopes and dreams. That's if you like beatboxing – don't if you hate it, obviously.

XXV

OWN IT, BABY, OWN IT

The victim mentality is the mother of all growth stunters. You have those who fight for themselves, winning victories over and over. Then there are others who just take continuous naps until life is finished, comatose with diazepam, television dramas and dysfunctional eating. Yes, if only you were a tortoise, the journey would be so much easier. If only you hadn't experienced [insert past issue here].

The 'casualty' complex tells you to run to another city for refuge. It tells you to fight against everyone else except yourself. It tells you that you're big boned, and that's why you're 29 stone. It tells you that your decision to steal another woman's husband was because he wasn't getting enough sex. Poor chap. It tells you that you don't have to make a decision today. It tells you decision-making is impossible. It tells you that God hasn't told you what your own heart wants. It tells you that it can wait till tomorrow, whatever 'it' is. It tells you that your finest isn't good enough. It tells you that you're incapable, you're unlovable, you were never worth it in the first place. It tells you the dog ate your homework. It tells you that you're on your period and that's why you stole someone's wallet. It lets medical diagnosis on the internet catalyse your hypochondria. It tells you to sign on the welfare for two years because a performing monkey called Jemima took the last job available in the entire planet.

It tells you that because of your past abuse, you should snort one more line. It tells you that you keep making mistakes, and that's why lethargy is your BFF. It tells you that you're not good with people. It tells you that women don't like you. Neither do men come to think of it. It tells you that you *try*, but to no avail. It tells you that others get lucky, but you probably won't. It tells you there's no expert help out there. It tells you there's no hope. It tells you that you never need to apologize, because it's not your fault.

It's exactly the reason why most counsellors, if they had the guts, would place a sign on their door in bold print shouting, 'You are your own problem'. But, of course, that's bad for business.

The martyr approach categorizes people into 'goodies' and 'baddies', falling into exaggerations that when they've ALMOST BEEN MURDERED BY BADDIES (someone interjected too fast on the motorway). They will find anyone willing to listen. Some use gossip as a great scape-goat to talk about their problem 200 times. They are the 'I cant's', 'I musts' and 'I don't knows' of society.

It is learnt, not bred but, you'll be delighted to know, it is possible to change. You may need a few people to kick you in the butt until you realize you're doing it, but if you want to resolve the reason why you keep messing everyone about in the dating game, or why you can't follow through, or why you are still in the same unhealthy relationship for another year because you're terrified of being eaten by giant tabby cats after taking a fall at home when you get to 38, then take notice: your life is screaming that you're playing victim.

I claim no immunity to becoming the whipping girl. I've signed the contract of being a lamb to the slaughter without even realizing. On a small scale, I've caused some conflict when I wouldn't forgive my boyfriend for lying (repeatedly).

'So then leave! After all you've experienced this already,' my friends would reply. Quite a simple solution you'd think.

'But. . . But . . . I have all my stuff at his house?'

'Why don't you get the dog to eat it?' my friends would respond.

Touché. Touché.

Instead of finishing and heading for pastures new, I'd stay in this lack of self-realization, gain some social sym-pathy, attaining a victimhood status. I'd also justify my

237

reasons for becoming a detective with my boyfriend's actions 'in case he did it again'.

Now I hate to make a similarity between myself and Hitler, but (mass murder and demonic hatred aside) the victim attitude of *Mein Kampf* was a perspective that made the Germans victims to their neighbouring countries. Placing aside for a moment his penchant for violent toy throwing, gas chambers and torture to suppress the minorities, the world war wasn't a result of power hunger, it occurred because Hitler was a paranoid victim.

And Hitler wasn't alone – they were all in on it: the Catholics and Protestants of Northern Ireland, the Serbians and the Croatians, Russia to Austria and the Sinhalese and Tamil in the Sri Lanka conflict.

I am not suggesting victim mentalities will end up in funding weapons of mass destruction, but you will have your own little duels; your emotions will be holding rifles ready to attack something that wasn't even there. The victim constantly looks for events, scenarios and misperceptions to back up how much it sucks for them.

The 'IT WASN'T ME' approach has been around since the days of Adam and Eve. Adam chucked the apple over his shoulder, shrugged his shoulders on interrogation, pointed his apple-smelling finger to Eve and shoved her into the gutter. She, in turn, then blamed the snake.

Sorrow is real and there is a place for it. I understand some people have not had healthy modelling for marriages, nor had any love from anyone of decent attitude or social grace since they were born, but your present was never meant to be led by your past – this is why you must dance on the past's grave.

Don't be an ambulance-chaser of drama. Maybe you, or someone you know, recently went through a break-up and so you ran to anyone else who was going through one, talking to them for hours on end or seeking some emotional pat on the back for what you're going through too.

I, too, sought affirmation from friends in the years of tragedy and loss. I certainly mentioned my grief enough in my daily conversation but I didn't sit down and process the pain; I took a couple of paracetamol for the headaches instead of seeking God for his comfort. I didn't want to be a victim, but still I was sharing the pain with everyone, seeking answers to fill the cracks of my heart, and at night I wasn't feeling any better.

I forgot one, pretty vital, thing. Heaven. I also forgot I was a powerful person, I forgot that God paid the highest price for me to be victorious in life. I forgot about the crucifixion. You know – that.

Regardless of struggles, I'm still powerful enough to decide how I will react. When I've confronted people on gossip, for example, they immediately blame an event, amnesia or a circumstance to justify talking about someone that was not their business. Or they ignore the confrontation all together, hoping it will go away. Both are powerless reactions.

As Christ walked through towns, speaking to the thousands, he was bombarded with people stretching out to touch him. People travelled for hundreds of miles purely on word of mouth PR, because he had something that nobody else had seen before.

Did he ever turn around to his disciples and say, 'I feel so used'? Did he complain of tiredness? Did he ever not stop for the one, because the previous group of people he taught rejected his works? No. He upped the ante, and got on with it.

Christ sucker-punched the victim mentality with a breath. When the fig tree didn't bear fruit, he cursed it.

He knew he was powerful. So he'd confront when someone attacked him, communicating in a way that vindicated the other person, but challenged their wrong beliefs. He wasn't scared of saying how he felt, he never buckled under a weight of fear. He still gave Judas bread at the Last Supper and washed his feet, despite betrayal.

Christ sucker-punched the victim mentality with a breath. When the fig tree didn't bear fruit, he cursed it. If someone was hurting, he'd show compassion, cry even, and fix the problem – no running, no complaining, no slander or blaming the circumstance. He showed more favour towards people who had *faith*, despite impasses, because he recognized that with faith they had hope. He wouldn't stop as much for the sceptics, those who spoke negatively or just plain moaned. He stopped for those who grabbed him and said, 'Help me change the record because I'm tired of it being scratched.'

To change there needs to be a waving goodbye to key elements. You have to take risks. You will have to be real to fall in love. Your attention and validation will have to come from God, not others. You will have to get out of the rocking chair of complaint. You will need to banish from your brain the 'buts' and listen to the advice of someone who does it better than you.

You think *The Secret* was revolutionary in its approach to positive thinking? It's been in scripture all along. See Philippians 2:14, 'Do all things without grumbling or moaning.' Quantum physics has been in existence since time began. The less grateful you are, the less you will declare over yourself that you can create a great life of abundant joy if you choose to do so.

You were saved before you were born, sweetheart. Salvation wasn't meant to be a walk in the park.

Untangle yourself from self-pity, regardless of everything you may have suffered. 'Oh but she doesn't know what it's like in my shoes.' You are right. I don't. But, even when I lost my father, both my uncles, my auntie, two friends in separate motorbike accidents – all

241

within eighteen months – I knew that someone else (God to you and me) had suffered pain watching his Son being tortured. Jesus was cut to shreds by naive commanders, butchered alive and, in those final moments he asked his Father, 'Why have you forsaken me?' With the reports of the skies turning black as Christ died during the sunlight hours of the day, I believe this was the moment when God faced his own hardest hour.

Yet the planet blames God for suffering, for our wounds, for 'not being there'. You were saved before you were born, sweetheart. Salvation wasn't meant to be a walk in the park. You will be challenged. You will face horrific pain. You will face temptations that try to distract you from loving yourself. You will be horrified by the acts of others. But you are powerful in all accounts. So take hold of your own choices, your own life and embody the very soul you were designed to own. And I say – bring it on.

Take ownership of your part in the game of life. Take ownership of your body, embrace your beauty rather than dispel its attraction. You are not a victim to *Cosmopolitan*, to your boyfriend, to the school bullying, to romantic comedies, to critique, to success, to fame, to your mother, your father, your brother, your sister, your own self. You are not the victim to your boss. You are not the victim to your credit card. You are not the victim to your sleep or vodka.

Give up the 'oh woe is me'. And today, remind yourself that you were chosen, saved against the lies that the enemy wanted you to come into agreement with. Accept that you are worth fighting for, that you have a God who seeks justice for you every day of your life. You may not see the proof of him doing so – in fact you'll probably argue that you can't. But you've no idea what attacks have come your way and what you've been protected from.

Christ is in you. Stop talking to God about fixing your problems, instead start talking to your problems directly.

Welcome to a new day, a day where owning your life and emotions embraces liberation on a colossal scale, taking you to the new panorama of God.

XXVI

SINGLEHOOD SLIPPERS

> 'But I would have you without carefulness. He that is unmarried careth for the things that belong to the Lord, how he may please the Lord.'
>
> (1 Corinthians 7:32, KJV)

If you're Diane Keaton, Coco Chanel or Condoleezza Rice, you have possibly escaped the judgement of never being married by distracting public opinion with your successful career. Coco 'never wanted to weigh more heavily on a man than a bird'[29] and I assume she was forgiven for never marrying the influential men she dated, because she designed the finest couture of her era. But if we have not married, nor have established an empire, does that mean there is something automatically wrong with us?

We were created for intimacy. Eve wasn't introduced just for her stylistic talents in fig leaf design, but for companionship. If we have a desire in our hearts to love and be loved, then it's a reality that we can't hide from. But must it govern us? When desperation begins to paint the town red, men can sense it, perpetuating the 'barren* status'.

I have friends – beautiful, wise, loving, hilarious friends – who have not found that worthy-of-a-lifetime chap. Especially if they have held out for a hot Kingdom marriage. There is a difference between marriage and Kingdom marriage. Both might be fruitful and multiply, but Kingdom marriage runs after an 'apostle' approach to relationship – infecting the community, the city, the world. Dramatic I know. The occurrences of such unions are miraculous events; the enemy doesn't want royal blood multiplying. It's too terrifying for him. MWAH HA HA HA.

When family and friends pressurize these delectable women, they're placing an ungodly agenda in the mix that makes said women feel inadequate. It seems that such people don't consider that the men they are trying to match-make single women with may be as suitable as a Subway sandwich to a gluten intolerant; they just want to get them wed.

My mother began saving for my wedding fund as soon as I turned 18. By my twenty-sixth year she expected there'd be enough in the ISA for a Phillipa Lepley gown and, by this point, a man to marry. When my first serious relationship ended when I was 23, she didn't give up hope

– but she did dip into the fund to fix a leak in the roof and bought a nice pair of sheepskin slippers.

'I just want to see you happy and settled,' was the whispered sentiment. For Mamma, being settled equalled happiness. Naturally, I made a point of introducing her to my friends who were already divorcing at 28. I began to lower my bets on men. If we do renounce our wants, we begin to compromise ourselves to fit the desires of wanting to just be with someone. We fight the urges to leave men that are not suitable for us.

When I confessed to my mum that things might have to end amicably in my most serious relationship to date, she replied: 'Do you think we should renovate the garage and make it into a study?'

The rest of the single female population are 'busying' their lives in order to avoid the starvation they appear to be suffering.

Returning home, embarrassingly, at 31 to live with my mother until I knew what my next career move was, I also closed down the business I owned with my now former boyfriend. My mum's reaction? She gave me a hug and passed me the Farrow & Ball catalogue.

When women hit their thirties there is a tendency for them to panic. Fear that they won't ever have children because the father with the goods never turned up sets in. They start to control and manipulate their current situation with a man, or begin hunting out of a need, not a want. The biological panic button gets pressed, the curse of Eve is faced and the author of time seems to get forgotten about in this carousel of Russian Baby Roulette.

So are there any women out there who are happy and single? I'm pleased to tell you there are, but they are few and far between. The rest of the single female population are 'busying' their lives in order to avoid the starvation they appear to be suffering.

Jane Austen, whose closest experience to marriage was being engaged to her best friend for twenty-four hours, wisely said, 'A lady's imagination is very rapid, it jumps from admiration to love, from love to matrimony in a moment.'[30]

She read my mother's emails – clearly. When I turned 32 my mother finally confessed, after seeing me refuse to settle for less than Kingdom marriage: 'I think your generation has it harder than we did. Financially we could all live alone, people fought for marriage motivated by synergy not megalomania. We didn't have Tumblr, and you don't have bands like the Beatles, never mind many men who would die for Jesus.'

The women I know who are happily single haven't necessarily chosen to be single forever, they just have a dedication to staying true to themselves until Mr Right not Mr Mediocre comes along. And I admire that. They don't spend their days 'cyber winking' to strangers online, drip-feeding themselves with affection from 'hook-up' apps – and they always duck when the wedding bouquet is thrown. Taking such a stand gives liberation to other twenty-first-century women who might feel the pressure to marry because not doing so would deem them 'unsuccessful' or 'unlovable'. The happy single women have fortunately risen above traditional expectations. They are not superfluous feminists, just women who enjoy their life and trust in God more than their comparative circumstances. They know they have a purpose; a husband and children are just extra blessings, should they come their way.

My friend, Miriam, comments: 'Ten years ago I didn't allow myself to say that I wanted to marry and have children. I'd reply, "If the Lord wills it." I was such a religious a***hole. That was out of fear and rejection. These days I'm happy to say I have a desire in my heart to raise children,

Marriage has a verisimilitude that cannot be falsified.

but ultimately it's so much more freeing to release that and give it back to the Lord than to try and conjure up results from those desires.'[31]

The fact is, there are many more singles in the world than you might think. For example, more than 56 million American adults have always been single; they represent roughly 60 per cent of the adult unmarried population.[32]

Even if people have found a beloved, they are not necessarily marrying them. The number of cohabiting unmarried partners increased by 88 per cent between 1990 and 2007, and 40 per cent of those split before marriage.[33]

Girlfriend, not everyone marries at 21. Half of the marriages that are embarked upon at an early age end in divorce and that's why marriage can never be a rushed decision. It isn't the Starbucks drive thru. Marriage has a verisimilitude that cannot be falsified. It was meant to be a one-time only deal; divorce is not the fall-back when you're faced with crunch time. Ask my divorced friends – it's such a painful process, up there on the stressometer with the death of a beloved.

People must be willing to die to the other, for better for worse, for richer for poorer, for awkward sex or ecstatic sex. On your wedding day your promise to God is that you are willing to lay down your life so that the two of you become one. Marriage only comes alive when people are willing to do that. You must die, in order to live. When I counsel girls one on one, the phrase 'I want to find my husband' is met with my retort of 'Why? Is it from a need or a want?' If it's a need, God may hold off until he thinks you can really handle the reality of marriage – the gutsy growth of sacrifice, compromise, honour and courage.

Marriage won't fix your weaknesses; it'll raise them to the surface. So why not try to enjoy the season you're in right now?

I was quite happy playing Odetta on vinyl while attempting the 'limbo' with my girlfriends, until someone gave me a free subscription to a Christian dating website that has made me question whether some of its members have seen the outdoors for the last fourteen years. Media, society and your neighbour might get challenged by your singleness. It may spirit-robbingly challenge them as they realize they must compromise and sacrifice more for family and covenant. Or they just fear you are lonely. The joy of having family within the church is that you're not. Chance to be lonely would be a fine thing – if the church is working well that is. Healthy churches will find a way to ensure singles are getting the same love as young families do. If leadership aren't offering events where you can all enjoy life with each other, then start them yourselves and make the choice to find joy amongst others who are single or dating.

Is our singlehood 'forgiven' if we serve the world to a more profound capacity? Maybe in the eyes of the fickle, but God never placed marriage in a commandment.

Companionship is available in the community, just not always romantically. It's desperation that I'm sick to the back canines of seeing. 'I have incredible friends all over the world, I have a fulfilling job, I have amazing experiences and opportunities (travel/work/fun), so I don't think I'm inadequate really. I don't think of joy/happiness as something that equates to your relationship status. One single girlfriend gave me this quote as a means of expressing her feelings on the matter: "Being single does not make you not-wonderful. A (married) friend recently told a (single) friend of mine that she hoped she knew she was amazing and that soon she'd find someone who'd tell her that. Oh, that's right. Single people of the world, remember this: in order to realize you're amazing, you must be told by someone – don't have confidence in yourself. Your amazing potential is simply waiting to be awakened by this glorious future partner of yours. For the record: that is not truth. No . . . you are of worth because YOU ARE of worth."'[34]

Is our singlehood 'forgiven' if we serve the world to a more profound capacity? Maybe in the eyes of the fickle, but God never placed marriage in a commandment, never cursed those who love themselves outside of a relationship.

Some of my single friends have adopted children and, in my humble opinion, the world needs more women like this. Biological yearnings are something to really look at carefully. Ask yourself, are they coming from a desire to be unconditionally loved? That is the story of so many of the 16-year-old teenagers I counsel who didn't get loved by a father in childhood (and beyond) so have sought it in the love from their own child. Does it come from a desire to be needed? Of course there are maternal wannabe mothers, and there are millions wanting to be married but, please, enjoy the singleness ride, no matter what age you are, until it is time for you to get off.

I refuse to define my worth by a rock on my finger, by a man who loves me in covenant. These are blessings, but I cannot be deflated when I don't have them. I am more concerned for the girl who doesn't give herself time to breathe between break-ups for fear of being alone. Or the girl who goes so far as to have an affair with a married man for the sake of being 'loved'.

Here's a caveat from yours truly: choosing to be single because marriage is daunting cannot be a justifiable reason to guard your solo lifestyle. Fear can never be a reason to avoid love. If you are as single as a dollar and are not looking for change, it could be for reasons of chemical make-up – no sex drive, no desires to marry, or you think you might have a tendency to murder in a red-blooded argument. The beauty of God is that you have free will. But never seek to look over the other side of the fence because of comparison or fear, just water where you're standing right now.

Being single isn't weak, nor is it failure; it means you are strong enough to wait for what you deserve and what you want.

I could have been married four times by now, if I'd chosen to settle for the man in front of me each time. But it would have been for a love without longevity, borne out of a decision based on what I knew about myself then and not who I am now. Within me there is a divine need to nourish my soul by serving God, but that's not to deny that my soul has intent to love a fine man and bring myself to the table for us as a team, not through a selfish solo gain. If I'm to be in relationship, it must bring glory to others – and to God. In order to be dutifully decent in romance, we need to be good at relationship on other levels, in community, in the workplace, in our families and in order to not be co-dependent. We need to be content with being alone and enjoy the season that we are in.

However, as happy single women, we must be careful to not become so used to our own ways that there is no lenience for a companion. It's easy to walk to McNally Jackson's bookshop in New York and dream away my day without having to think about anyone else, other than the friends who ring me, the men who want to date me (no no) and the purpose I'm delightfully walking in.

If you're reading this still in your pyjamas because nobody loves you romantically, then get up, sweetheart. There's an entire world that you were created to succour, with or without a husband. Procreation was not your only job requirement, because any female post-puberty can do that, and social services will be the first to tell you – some don't do it well.

In New York and London, the average age to marry is a lot later these days – mid to late thirties. Some of my friends in their early forties have just found their significant other, bringing so much to the relationship because they really knew who they were beforehand. The 39-year-old fashion editor who thought she'd never find a man suitable, married at 40. A 41-year-old TV news reporter who lived between New York and San Francisco, found a man who was more successful than her (therefore not intimated by her) and gave birth to her first child at the age of 42. In both of these cases, the women loved life and led a fulfilled lifestyle, with friends, purpose, joy and contentment. If the guy came along, great; if he didn't, it wasn't the end of the world.

Within your single soul, nothing is impossible, so go grab the panache of life. Flying solo should never be underestimated, it should be celebrated.

Kingdom marriage is a miraculous gift that will take you to new depths. Kingdom singlehood is as treasured in the eyes of the Lord. If you abuse your solo season with a belligerent need to be saved by another (did we miss the part about already being saved?) you'll miss the opportunities to experience the divine, the expeditions that will melt you, the assignments that your Father may require you to do while you can focus purely on him.

Be joyful. You have no limitations. Within your single soul, nothing is impossible, so go grab the panache of life. Flying solo should never be underestimated, it should be celebrated, especially if it's a foundation to a more interesting you.

'I didn't get married until I was 50,' a quote came up on an online feed with the picture of a woman who'd clearly led the wild lifestyle of an artisan. 'I think it finally happened because I stopped thinking it was possible. Before I gave up, I was putting so much pressure on myself and measuring every man I'd meet. It's not natural to begin a relationship with such a long-term view. When I met my husband I wasn't looking past that afternoon.'[35]

So do me a favour, would you, darling? Be radical. Be a strong woman that goes low, gets humble in love, waiting for no one, to succeed in the purpose God's given you.

Go on. Be daring. Don't wait for the man. Wait upon God. Find the season that he has given you in your present moment, rather than wishing upon a star for something different. Acceptance is part of the key to contentment. He has held such special moments for you to treasure in your single years, so instead of living in a constant self-indulgent psychosis of desperation, waiting for a man to come save the day, make God proud by embracing the elements that have already been given to you.

Wouldn't it be a shame to miss our lives entirely because we wanted our own agenda to be met before his?

XXVII

BECAUSE YOU'RE WORTH IT

'Let us always meet each other with a smile, for the smile
is the beginning of love.'

(Mother Teresa)

As I've buttered the pages of this book with traces of learned wisdom and personal trials, I realize it's easy to make this whole process too complex, over-analytical, tiring your eyes with too much to consider.

Principles of loving mean nothing without personal encounters of God's love. These themes will not get under your skin unless you hear the real stories where the superheroes of our generation – the men who owned a pair (sorry mother) – showed the world that love conquers every time. But even then, such men are inaccessible if you don't believe you deserve them, so the magnetism starts when you truly begin to honour yourself first.

I gain insight about what version of love I deserve from the 5.1 surround-sound of words emanating from my tender-hearted friends who love their wives endlessly, effortlessly. These men, and my other brothers in Christ, honour my heart with no plans for selfish gain, with communication of the highest standard, layering it with a protection that would cover me from being harmed by others and from their own desires.

The magnetism starts when you truly begin to honour yourself first.

These vignettes will challenge, hopefully, the most pessimistic of minds regarding Kingdom-cultured men.

From the windmills in heaven comes a breathtaking fearlessness pouring itself onto men throughout the world. Men of honour, men of chutzpah, men who fight and fight one more time for their girl. They are the Pralines and Crème variety of the male species – my favourite flavour. Men who place themselves under the wings of God's protection: their justice hearts ignite parliamentary movements, their compassion disables the broken, their tenderness challenges the most stubborn of our species. They do not weaken in storms – they embrace them. They giggle in the face of danger as they trust in their history with the Lord. They are unoffended by your meltdowns, your illnesses, your own storms, your menstrual cycle. For, by the morning, they give account to God on how well they've looked after his daughters. They need not manipulate, charm or seek emotional need from others, for they are steadfast in him and him alone.

While I was writing this chapter, an incredible man – 6 ft 4 in, handsome, highly intelligent, stylish, comedic gent with a penchant for the odd mansion – drove eight hours to arrive on my doorstop late at night, after a dream he had about marrying me, confessing his 'huge crush'. It was the most awesome term of affection I'd encountered for years, because it came with an emotional risk, placing pride in the glove compartment for that night. He had no idea about any of my affections after all. We talked (about God) for hours, laughed in bucket loads. Easy – just as it should be. I thanked him for the gesture, for his gutsy honesty and for being a true man that just went with a hunch.

So we flew to Vegas and I married him, with a man called Jeff as our witness, outside a kebab shop. The End.

Gosh you know me so well – no, there was no wedding.

The amount of self-love we've invited into our Monday to Sunday life reflects in the men around us. I'm finishing *The Virgin Monologues* with this chapter to ensure you own a new perspective, an optimism, proving your faith resounds in God wanting to fulfil all your desires.

The moments when men pull out all the stops are truly valuable accounts. They plump up hope, smashing the lie that says that gallant men don't exist any more. So let this renew your mind; if just for a few minutes.

A woman deserves to be celebrated and men are not to be placed in the 'idiot' folder. It's time to honour them again, their efforts and their real wish to show affection.

The real honour is revealed in the little things. Love notes left on your windscreen, carved in the snow, flown through the air. Your favourite meal waiting for you at home, the surprise trips, the interrupted sentences to compliment you. That limited-edition vinyl of James Brown you've been searching for for years. The treasure hunts with terms of affection as your prize. The wrap-around hugs that rinse out your bad day.

But then there's the fight. While cowards don't fight, they run, it's in the fight that the superheroes of the twenty-first century show their magnificence. You can have all the niceties from John O'Groats to Lands End, but without fight, longevity's throat gets cut. It's here where the real, Christ-love surfaces. The reconciliation when she or he has messed up. The fight for loving on purpose, regardless of what s/he can give at the time.

We live in an era where we believe that if we aren't functioning on all cylinders consistently, he's going to leave. We can't be ill, we can't have a rough day, we can't air our concerns in case it causes a sprint-like effect in his response.

Yet if you switch off the TV for an hour, you'll find the husbands I found: the man who remained faithful for nine years in a sex-less marriage because his wife had ovarian cancer. He remained committed all the way through to her death, taking care of the three kids.

The man who looked after his girlfriend of eight months through four spinal operations, while she was high on morphine and, to top it off, comforted her through bereavement after her mother died.

The man who confessed an affair to his wife, and, instead of leaving for the stereotype secretary, fought to win back the love they once had, confessing his wrongdoing in front of his entire church, asking for forgiveness and for support for his hero – his wife. Their marriage strengthened, becoming better than it was before, inspiring other couples not to give up on their marriages.

Heaven is watching for you to take your next move and can't align with anything outside of your original design.

The man who placed her career in front of his (need we look further than the Duke of Edinburgh?), walking behind his Queen for the sake of his country.

Each of these men place the love of others above selfish gain. They consciously act on what is right for their lady without moaning.

Don't think for one second that you can't have the finest of God's faculty. You can't change the world with love if you're doing the same as everyone else. That doesn't spark inspiration. It doesn't get the angels' attention. Heaven is watching for you to take your next move and can't align with anything outside of your original design. Seek the radical stories and use them for inspiration.

Whether you're single and happy, single and sad, self-loathing or a girl that just wants to get it right, take note of what you've been given right now. No comparison. No pessimism based on your past – did you not read the above? The calibre of fine males has not become extinct, exchanged for the needy zombie that cares more about his property value or that line-manager promotion. Focus on you, your God and your purpose.

Within the gratitude for what you have right now, joy will rise in your decision to make your life a deluxe version. Value will marinate the very relationships you attract, and going solo should never be underestimated. The transformation of your mind's eye is the powerful potion to eradicate the pewter perspective you once had about yourself and welcome in the gold.

Believe in people again, live no more in reaction to what you've experienced before. Retain a new truth, the one in the Gospel, the one that radically transforms lives from mess to marvellous. God's waiting for you to show up. He's waiting for you to represent your relationship in your every day. He's ready to show you things you've never dreamed of: people who will blow you away, healing, signs and wonders that magnify what the real fear of the Lord is – and that's just how good God is. His is a love that ignites passions and creates new stories, new tales with happier endings for the next generation.

You were made different for a reason. For a world-need.

There are a thousand ancestors gunning for you, and you alone, to win in the war of good and evil. There are a million more, waiting for you to take your place with confidence so that heaven can invade earth with a love so potent, it changes people forever.

It can only happen when you align with the very government you came from, before your time on earth. You've come to fulfil assignments, not just to procreate, nor even marry – but to embrace the individualized DNA that only you have. You were made different for a reason. For a world-need. Just as a butterfly flapping its wings in South America can affect the weather in Central Park, you too, will change the course of history forever, even if it were as simple as loving your neighbour as yourself. So love until it aches.

Love with the understanding you were intended to live with, limitless moments of exhilaration, ecstatic laughter and tears of joy, rained on by love. In this world is a warfare of good and evil, of over-the-top opinion and meekness, of courage and fear, of tradition and post-modernism, of past hurts and future redemption. So whose side will you take? For you must take one. One involves being the dynamite bombshell that doesn't care for society's swaying opinion, the other may not ever find herself amongst all that she's been told to be.

He's waiting for you. He's always been waiting for you.

Because, sweetheart, you're worth it.

You've always been worth it.

Every.

Single.

Time.

CARRIE'S PRACTICAL POINTERS

- Victim mentality is one of the most debilitating mind-sets. Get strong. Get real and allow only a certain amount of time to wallow, be sad, *process* the pain. Then it's time to let it go. **It's easier to blame circumstances, than to trust again and take risk, but risk you must – in order to obtain freedom.**

- Singledom is not failure, is not finality, it is a season. Embrace it, enjoy it. You may only have this time, for you never know what is coming around the corner. **A relationship does not define your worth, God does.**

- **Surround yourself with people who set healthy standards in their own romantic relationships,** who influence you in the belief that honourable men are out there, ensuring you won't settle.

- Above all, your faith in God will be reflected in the worth you place on yourself. **If you degrade or put yourself down, you immediately insult God's work – the creation of you.** If you find it hard to take a compliment, or can't get out of the rut of self-deprecation, ask yourself why you do not own the gorgeous design that you are.

- Life is meant to be joyful. **You are a powerful woman whose fulfilment shouldn't rely on people's actions or people's opinions.** Embrace your unique design, and embrace your worth to return back to hope, optimism and a heavenly, Kingdom lifestyle.

EPILOGUE

I'm not a virgin.
I'm not an atheist.
I'm in love with God.
I'm in love with love.
I invite intimacy and the fans of it to my home.
I am full of justice-fight, marinated in grace.
I am a player of my imagination.
I'm a treasurer of my imagination.
I don't watch porn.
I am still provocative.
I am less confused.
I am a dancer.
I am not a performer.
I am a writer.
I love the camera – especially when it doesn't love me.
I am a better friend.
I am a better girlfriend.
I still love them after a break-up.

Epilogue

I am a daughter.
I am still opinionated.
I am trusting more.
I am not dishonest.
I am honest in love.
I am the honey to his beehive.
I am the refrigerator to his milk.
I refuse to be a coward.
I am still a feminist in male-love clothing.
I am a happy singleton and a grateful lover.
I am a journalist for national magazines.
I am an author.
I still obsess over Valentino and Oscar De La Renta as much
as Neo-Darwinism.
I am not defined by my Manolos, but by the eyes of God.
I drink from the well of love, with no wish to die.
I fear God's power, not man's.
I trust myself.

Today, I don't mind being labelled. And neither should you. As long as we don't define our self by the labels. I do refuse to be a statistic, and I enjoy the challenge of proving them wrong. For society might create patterns of behaviour, but we're bigger than that, because God is bigger than that.

Just as I've seen the power of the word 'Christ' transform the most hopeless, and as heaven made a home in you, so, too, are your words powerful – over yourself, over others, over life. And I always choose life. My question is – will you?

If the world expects loving actions, we have to raise the standard again, we have to stay in relationship, even when it's tough. Especially when it's tough. We have to embrace love on a whole other level.

Yes it starts with us, with self-love – that's the basic message. But this has to start from outside of our own arrogance, outside of our limited wisdom. We must reach out to a much more powerful entity. I'd rather rely on him who is more powerful than the solar system than myself – as I'm the one who could get crushed by a golf cart if I don't look both ways.

Emotional intelligence only buys you so much. Emotional maturity buys you a little more. But an encounter with Christ pays for everything, even the priceless. You weren't a broken Christian, your eyes were focusing on the wrong things. In the dalliance of life, you just needed to lighten up your soul and scrape out all the crap. And as we will all make mistakes for the rest of our lives, it's how we clear up the mess that's important.

So let's not hide behind perfection, nor expect everyone else to. Let's not judge. Let's not be the victim. Let's not think we have more favour if we read more of the Bible. Let's get real with God. Let's be ourselves, like he's been asking us to be for centuries. Let's become famous for loving radically. Not in a matter of random acts of kindness, but in continuous acts of kindness. Consistency is far more unusual these days.

Leaders, get vulnerable and share your life lessons, we need them to make the church relative again. Let no one in society be excluded. Parents, let no subject be avoided, no matter how uncomfortable it makes you feel. We need leaders, mentors, fathers and mothers who aren't afraid to challenge, and aren't afraid to love outrageously. This isn't the stiff-upper-lip era; this is the era for no-holds-barred.

Whether it's standing in the Sistine Chapel in the Vatican, holding a leper in India, having the police called to an apartment in Tribeca, New York, because a hundred of us couldn't get enough of God that night; his love is expressed in everything, anything. Even in the midst of war, tsunamis and our bad decisions in free will, God shows up in the thousands of people who fly to rescue and feed the desperate.

It's so easy to lose track of the importance of life or how short it is, so treat it kindly, with reverence, with gratitude and with a smile. Don't wait for your exit, to find out the real answers.

You were meant to be here, for such a time as this, so fight – and fight for a love-filled life.

ENDNOTES

1 My blog can be found at herglassslipper.co.uk
2 Sue Manwaring, Global Legacy, California, in conversation, 2013.
3 nobelprize.org/nobel_prizes/medicine/laureates/1977/yalow-speech
4 Bill Johnson, Senior Pastor, Bethel Church, California, taken from a 2013 sermon.
5 Claire Heydon, friend, personal trainer, wife, mother, worship leader, in conversation, 2013.
6 A journal entry of mine from 2013.
7 Katie Veach, spiritual mentor, friend, mother and wife, in conversation.
8 Bill Cahusac, GB leadership team for 24-7 Prayer Movement and vicar at Holy Trinity Brompton, London, in conversation in 2013.
9 'Britain's Part Time Wives' by Jamie Dettmer: thedailybeast.com/witw/articles/2013/08/05/britain-s-muslim-communities-see-rise-in-multiple-marriages-as-career-women-seek-part-time-husbands
10 Markus Kirwald, business entrepreneur and friend. In conversation in New York, 2013.

Endnotes

11 William Shakespeare, *Hamlet*, Act 3, Scene 1.

12 Kris Vallotton, Lecture in Bethel School of Supernatural Ministry, 2014.

13 brainyquote.com/quotes/quotes/s/stevejobs416876

14 Used in a sermon at Holy Trinity Brompton, but the story can be found online at josephylee.org/diegain

15 Used by Nelson Mandela in his 1994 inaugural speech.

16 fathersloveletter.com/text – based on Psalm 139:15–16.

17 From Jon Van Epp, *How to Avoid Falling in Love With a Jerk*, (McGraw Hill, 2007).

18 In conversation in New York, 2013.

19 ncbi.nlm.nih.gov/pubmed/9868824

20 brainyquote.com/quotes/quotes/p/plato392892

21 Melody Beattie, *Codependent No More: How to Stop Controlling Others and Start Caring for Yourself* (San Francisco: Hazelden Foundation, 1992).

22 Anne, mother, lecturer, business consultant, in conversation in 2013.

23 From Jon Van Epp, *How to Avoid Falling in Love With a Jerk*, (McGraw Hill, 2007).

24 dailymail.co.uk/home/you/article-1346813/The-flip-1960s-sexual-revolution-We-paid-price-free-love

25 Ruth Atkins, 29, friend, in conversation in California, 2014.

26 *GQ* magazine, '10 Reasons Why You Should Give Up Porn': gq.com/blogs/the-feed/2013/11/10-reasons-why-you-should-quit-watching-porn

27 Anthony Hilder, life coach, writer, husband, in conversation, 2014.

28 John-Paul Gentile, musician and songwriter for Bethel Music, California, in conversation in 2014.

29 Laura Jacobs, 'The Enduring Coco Chanel' in *The Wall Street Journal* online: online.wsj.com/news/articles/SB1000142405 29702043239045770385728186012252

30 Jane Austen, *Pride and Prejudice* (Darcy to Miss Bingley, chapter 6).

31 Miriam Dumlao, 29, single (and awesome), in conversation in New York.

32 US Census Bureau. 'America's Families and Living Arrangements: 2007', taken from unmarried.org/statistics/

33 'America's Families and Living Arrangements: 2007'.

34 Friend, in conversation.

35 Woman quoted on Humans of NY Instagram feed.

GLOSSARY

Alexander McQueen An angel disguised as a fashion designer. Recently passed away, but the finest British designer (Vivienne Westwood aside) to date.

Aung San Suu Kyi Burmese opposition political activist. She remained under house arrest in Burma for almost fifteen of the twenty-one years from 20 July 1989 until her most recent release on 13 November 2010, becoming one of the world's most prominent political prisoners. She was awarded the Nobel Peace Prize in 1991.

Black Thunder Babe An interesting career choice I made for radio. I was a promotional girl wearing a black bomber jacket and far too much pink lipstick. My main job was to deal out cash in random car parks – the first people to find me after my location was announced on radio would get cold hard cash. It was terrifying and glorious and all for a £5.97 per hour wage.

Balatron Another word for buffoon.

Chagrin Distress or embarrassment at having failed. That's not a term we'll use for you. No no.

Choos Nickname for Jimmy Choo shoes.

Chris Pine The question is not who is he. The question is why don't you know who this man is? Hmm? Should be the second name you know after Jesus Christ. (Films such as: *Star Trek*, *Z for Zachariah*.) In short, God was having a good day when he designed Chris Pine.

Cristina Fernandez De Kirchner President of Argentina. Fierce too.

Emmeline Pankhurst A British political activist and leader of the British Suffragette movement who helped women win the right to vote. She was, as the locals say, 'bad ass'. End of.

Eros, Storge, Philia and Agape The four loves: *eros* – romance; *storge* – affection; *philia* – friendship; *agape* – unconditional love.

Ezer Kenegdo Eve was given to Adam as 'helpmeet' or, in the Hebrew, *ezer kenegdo*. Scholarly translations will advise that it means less helper, rather rescuing, saving or filling in the places that Adam could not manage. But there are many references in the Bible where great women brought strength to the nations, or were not married and still remained favoured in God's eyes.

Fatal Attraction Quite a disturbing movie in which Glenn Close performs her finest hour after murdering a bunny rabbit and placing it on the stove of the man she admires. I'd have suggested giving them a nice Tag watch, but there we go. She was a little disgruntled after he decided to not leave his wife for her. The film is awkward on many levels and should you be thinking about exploring the world of adultery – watch this and you'll think twice.

FOMO 'Fear of Missing Out' slogan for the young and hip members of society. I am not one of them.

Heather Mills Interview I met this lady when I was 21, when she was engaged to Paul McCartney. What a lovely lady. Not brilliant at handling a divorce, though. But hey, I've never been through one – so I'm not to judge. The interview was 'viralled' around the globe as she disclosed probably a little too much detail about her split with Macca, becoming so emotional on national

UK television she began to talk in a high-pitched voice – even the TV presenter interviewing her felt out of her depth. It was the talk of the office and many women wanted to run to her rescue.

High Woo/High I Terms used from the personality test 'Strength Finder' and DISC tests. High Woo = charming, knows how to entice a crowd. High I = a person of high influence.

Jared Leto The most beautiful Adonis of the twenty-first century. Came to fame in a TV series called *My So-Called Life*. In fact I had a relationship with a boy for two years purely because he looked like him. It's extreme I know. But by golly. He's beautiful. Even at the age of 42.

Kate Spade Clothing and accessories designer, bold in colour and design. Not as pricey as Prada.

LBD If God were to pick the perfect Little Black Dress, it would probably be up-lit in the window of Jeffreys store in New York's meat-packing district, potentially with its own humming theme tune, because little black dresses (obviously not too little to display some ladylike modesty, darling) make one's soul sing.

Glossary

Miu Miu Only the craziest and most delectable shoe and accessory designer one could place one's pastel eyes on. Oh mother, hand me a cold towel.

Moleskine All art directors and copywriters with any taste will be found walking around with one of these notebooks in tow. Why Moleskine? Well, darling, the pages just fall where told to, the texture is smooth and you can have a hard or soft leather cover. The more you wear one in, the more it feels like woollen slippers for the fingertips.

Monmouth Coffee House The finest coffee in London, found in a pop-up shop near London Bridge and another just off Neal Street in Covent Garden – go earlier than lunchtime, unless you like being crushed in small spaces.

OPI Delicious brand of nail varnish that offers so many ranges in colour, it makes you wonder just how many colours there possibly can be on the planet. Found in most good salons. If God were to recommend nail varnish (believe it or not I think he actually likes to be involved in all things, even these girly details) then he would probably recommend OPI.

Philophobe A person scared of falling in love. You know the sort.

Question Time A topical debate show broadcast by the BBC in the UK.

Quoob Urban dictionary – Jerk.

Shoulding Term first referenced by my friend Melissa Casey, whose father would constantly remind her to stop 'shoulding' herself. Refers to placing too much demand and pressure on one's everyday life. The importance of going gently on oneself.

SG 0418+5729 Star A star that has the strongest magnetic field in the galaxy (as we know it).

Sleepless in Seattle The classic 1993 rom-com, where Meg Ryan and Tom Hanks fall in love before emails came into action.

Soul Ties The Bible doesn't use the term soul tie, but it speaks of them when it talks about souls being knitted together, becoming one flesh, etc. A soul tie can serve many functions, but, in its simplest form, it ties two souls together in the spiritual realm. Some can be healthy ties. Others can be unhealthy, especially outside of marriage. They can be made through sex, close relationships (King David and Jonathan had a close relationship – so it doesn't necessarily pertain to just opposite sexes) or vows and commitments.

Spanx If you've never heard of these, then I may just be about to change your life. A woman, now a billionaire thanks to her daydream, invented the modern-day girdle, which sucks and tucks in all manner of love handles. It's been a great friend to many of my girls. Best not to use one on your wedding night though.

Ted Bundy Not someone you would have wanted over for afternoon tea. Listed as one of the top serial killers in history – 1946–1989. American serial killer, rapist, kidnapper. Killed more than thirty women and girls. We'll leave it there. *Shudders*

Tony Montana Al Pacino's famous character in the movie *Scarface*. Not someone you'd want to marry. But he does come up with a cracking line.

Two Fingers for Dessert Slang for bulimia. First learnt by a fellow acting friend at university – when we were all at it.

United Colors of Benetton Poster Famous for their advertising campaigns and billboard posters highlighting the ethnic diversity in our many skin colours across the world. There are often controversial propaganda campaigns attached to this clothing company.

ACKNOWLEDGEMENTS

Without my publisher, Malcolm Down, being offended by the first ever blog post he discovered, this book wouldn't have materialized. So thank you for overriding your offence and powering through to give me a voice. Your advocacy of me has often left me bashful. I'm humbled by your encouragement and belief in me. You've become a great friend and your trust in me has built a new outlook.

Amy Boucher Pye who dressed the Royal Robe with such elegance as I humbly watched like a lady in waiting. Your ability to overview God's assignment in this, along with carrying grace for my experiments in risqué wordage has been wonderful.

Rachel Cloyne for embracing my rather specific art direction in illustration with such seriousness – I'm so glad Malcolm found you.

Claire Musters, whose patience and diligence has provided such a grace towards me, despite me walking so close to the edge on occasion, you trusted the way. For your attention to insane detail while holding onto my voice. Thank you!

Kate Beaton, for your brilliant honesty and enigmatic encouragement. For your marketing expertise and ability to adapt to change management!

Lawrie Stenhouse, the man of whom my first impression was of him joyfully problem-solving the dilemma of dropping his keys down a drain. 'Now there's a happy man who could promote my book,' I thought. Thankful for you.

Friends and Family

To Hayley Sims (Goldilocks) and Minki Design for your creativity and generosity on Her Glass Slipper, and for your friendship since we were 11 years old. From Stamford, to Brixton, to Cheltenham, from cigarettes to my purity, you've watched it all and remained consistently loving.

Malcolm Croft – I am forever humbled by your talent, by your support to keep me trying and for your incredible skills in hoopla. Thank you for loving me as a friend for all these years. Very few men can make me cry-laugh like you can.

Acknowledgements

To those whose conversations inspired many of these musings: Carly Allen (for your consistent support), Laura Corcoran, Johanna Young, Brendon De Puma, Fabiano and Claire Altamura, Katherine Romp, Danielle Baker, Tilly Hawkins, Megan Cotton, Erica Lucha, Tyler Lydell, Joshua Woodward, Mark Dombowsky, Barbara Ramseier, Vanessa Brown, Matt Murnan, Malcolm Crow, Barbara Miller, Sheva Nickravesh, Katrina Stevenson, Shaun Buckley, Emma Christina, Ryan Morley Male, Carol and Aidan Haylock, Kami Witte, Rachel Wood and Matt Sanderson (for your artistic inspiration), The Sprenger Family, The Peterson Family, Melissa Casey, Hayley Braun, David Norona, Nicola Sheehan, Emily and Mary Williams, Eddy Martinez, Alex Douglas, Johanna Young, Jo Cheng, Ben Byler, Jamie Warner, Rachel Molano, Helen Morkel Walton, Suzy Bergman, Claire and Luke Christian-Farman, Sarah Ferrera, Rob Carr, Savannah Cove, Jane McKeever, Lizzy Cook, Shayla Brown, Zachary Beukema, Katharine Welby-Roberts and afternoon tea at Lambeth, Sophie and Greg Jones, Victoria Gottschalk (you can thank me with chocolate éclairs), Milly and Harry Colvin, Marina Tucker, Jane and Doug Henderson (for your continual life-long support) Maggie Ritchie, Abby Heywood, Brandon Schweinier, Ashton Fullmer, Jocelyn Castro and Jason Segel.

To Pete Vickers, for those talks, for your ears (not physically but for their ability to listen) and your smile. For dragging me to the prayer house when I felt so overwhelmed with workload. I adore your compassion and honesty. For your vision of everyone having the right to Chronicle.

To Victoria White for giving me airtime to talk about Jesus in *Company Magazine*.

To Sarah Barnes, the one powerhouse I've always loved working for. Thank you for your friendship, mentorship and laughter.

To Clare Murwill (and Chloe Heth) for introducing me to Bethel in the first place. For your love, Clare, throughout this year; your heart shines so bright. Thank you for loving me regardless of my life and its style in the past. You loved me without judgement, without question, with nothing but joy.

To my family: Clare and Dick Saunders, Ian, Alison, William and Nem James. Thelma James. Jane and Jim! And the 10,000 horses. To my late Uncle David Lloyd, Uncle Christopher James and Grandpa James: I miss you. Utterly. Thank you for your provision, for your limitless humour, for your love. For your patience. I only hope you see the outcome of your investment and time in me.

To my soul sistas Andrea Boden, Susie Keegan, Jude Trenier. No matter what, I can always trust you to tell me my fly is undone *after* I've delivered a sermon. Your hope in my future and my men have always kept me smiling. I can be myself with you, while I stare at the Lord.

Junior Garr, you blessed me that night the cops were called in to that loud worship session. New York will never look the same to me. Gramercy Hotel, you and me and a piano in the room finds me giddy. Your voice is to be treasured forever.

Julian Springer, thanks for 'being in it for the long haul'. England needs men like you, who yearn to grow, to love and to be fearless. It's been beautiful, Jules.

Contributors

To Sue Manwaring, the woman who makes me wait with bated breath for the punch lines and tears at the redemption stories. Thank you for your time and trust.

Abi Classey, thanks for your words of love, honesty and Cosmopolitans amongst the skyline and introducing me to the men of New York City. May your vulnerability be forever powerful.

Miriam Dumlao, heart-melting thanks for your dulcet tones, the flowers, the love, the letters of encouragement and for a depth in friendship that brings me to my humble knees. I've never seen such love and joy.

Brittany Karen, thank you, sweet lady, for lending me the 'writing apartment' on Fifth Avenue, New York, for speaking into my life and for burning with a passion and justice that feeds my female soul.

Markus Kirwald, such gratitude for our coffees, encouragement and honesty in NYC movements. That city is blessed to have you; keep on healing the deaf, the broken, comforting the lost and spreading the glory.

Ben Decker – what a life you've led. It's great to have someone like you to encourage this message. Thank you for taking the time to endorse it.

Ruth Atkins, thank you for stretching my brain membranes just a little more. Your love is infectious. For that weekend in Napa and that moment in that designer boutique. Your cheerleading inspires me to be a better friend.

To all the anonymous contributors: your vulnerability was inspirational. Thank you for the emails, dinners with incredible storytelling and such brutal honesty. You're bringing breakthrough. I repeat – you're bringing breakthrough!

Acknowledgements

To Claire and Brad Heydon, thanks for your love and kindness amongst the community and loving equally all those around you without judgement.

Anthony Hilder, thank you for your writing heart, wisdom, wit and generosity. May this be your year!!

Erica Greve – the female William Wilberforce – you're the inspiration that makes us fight harder. Here's to more victories in the battle against sex trafficking.

Melissa Iford – your heart and your incredible journey, from the early years to your freedom years, makes you a hero to many of us. I could have written a whole book on you alone.

Mentors

Superhero thanks to my pastor Jake Veach for showing me how a man who really loves the Lord, really loves his wife. For teaching me about Kingdom dating. I only wish I had met you both sooner. To his insanely brilliant wife Katie Veach, for showing me finally how a true love for God manifests itself in one of my favourite marriages I've ever witnessed close up. I owe much of these polished sentences to nights of coffee, tears and your storytelling. When I see a woman climb across ten chairs just to say they love you,

I can't help but want to follow your gift of encouragement. It's incomparable to anything else I've ever seen. And I've seen a fair bit.

To Bill and Nici Cahusac (my spiritual parents in the UK), for sharing your story and for your time while you change the city of London. Your marriage provides great protection and self-belief to many of those I love.

To Beverly and Pete Williams (my spiritual parents in the US), who stopped me from leaving Bethel twenty minutes after I arrived. Thank you for reminding me of my worth. My life out here wouldn't be the same without your family love and belief in freedom.

Gabe (the kindest Mexican in the land) and Leah Valenzuela, thank you for covering me in Chihuahuas in the long hours of the night. Your hospitality helped me find my own voice no matter the adversity. Thank you also for teaching me about the fear of others, and how to kick its butt with 100 lb weights. To serve you is a blessing. Your leadership and family have taught me a whole new side of love.

To Bill Johnson, for reminding me of Habakkuk 2:2, Psalm 48 and Isaiah 30:8. For reminding me never to sit on the fence in fear of having an opinion. Sincere thanks for your precious time and encouragement in my writing, and for feeding an apostolic view of the prostitute at Jesus' feet. You're right, Jesus did do it for her. Our lives have found liberty, thanks to your fathering. Thank you for reminding me in conversation that love is brutally simple.

Special thanks

To WD, the man who loved me and still shows such kindness today, thank you for being in my life. For showing me what fighting for a woman looks like, for your honour and respect even after we had to part after five years. I am so blessed to have met you, for you set a great standard for the Mr Steadfast to come. Thank you for reminding me of my worth. Thank you for being, above all, a wonderful friend to this day.

Thanks to my 'Connect 4' girls:
Leah Sookoo: for your eye for detail in my words, and in my heart. For bringing a poetry to the mundane and Odetta to my vinyl.

Lindsay Berumen: for your tears of love and your purity of heart. Thank you for being forever loyal, forever considerate and forever diplomatic.

Ruth Blackhar: pour tes rires d'honnêté, ton coeur de justice qui n'est pas facilement influencé par une doctrine quelconque. Pour tes chuchotements en français si tu es en désaccord, oh combien cela apporte de la joie à mon âme, et pour m'avoir emmené dans les rues de Paris et de t'être excusé pour mon manque de français.

To all three of you, for teaching me intimacy. For your patience as I hibernated to write, for your encouragement and your laughter as I read these pieces to you at night. For covering me, when it felt no one else was for a month or two. Here's to the first of many, many years of friendship.

Kim (and husband Dave Conlon): for your beautiful level-headed rationale, for your encouragement and for your lifelong friendship. You're the finest parents your children could dream up. Truly.

To Charlie Calton-Watson (and husband Andy Calton): what glorious friendship you've shown me. What faith you've had in me. From playing Twister through to working in the marketing department with biker boys. You've been one trustworthy friend, loving me so unconditionally that I can't imagine my life without your voice. Here's to you, the family that raised you, your husband and that leaky punt in Duddington.

To Dawn O'Porter (and husband Chris O'Dowd), for loving me unconditionally. Dawn, it was your belief in my writing back in 2010 that led me to here. Thank you for your incredible dedication to friendship, for reaching out when the going got ridiculous and for trusting me with your furry children. For your loyalty, it still works with you and me. And it's beautiful. Marrying you both illegally was one of the best days of my life.

John-Paul Gentile: the man who sees the veins on the leaves before the trees. My musical maestro – making my fingertips weep; my words to your rhythm: a perfect combination while I write. Your editing, your critique, your wisdom and your experience in life melts me. Thank you for welcoming me to the Gentile family (Jared Gentile, Justin Gentile, LaChelle Gentile, Damian Gentile and your incredible parents Joseph and Patricia Gentile) and for teaching me another perspective of what real men look like. You're worth a billion more words than this paragraph. You love without condition, without expectation, all while you skip to the Lord's heartbeat. I've never seen love in the way that you do it, so here's to many more years of you in my life. The greatest bringer of joy.

To organizations

Bethel School of Supernatural Ministry, California
Care Confidential
CareNet
Freedom Church, Red Bluff

Holy Trinity Brompton
Stamford Free Church
The Leprosy Mission

The finest: my parents

To my mother, Revd May Lloyd, Mrs Tiggywinkle, my ever-consistent *auxilium*. You are the one who comes without comparison in *agape* love. You have saved more lives than I could ever hope to do. You changed the Baptist movement to allow female ministers in the eighties and still you inspire us today. From the puppet shows you acted out when I was 6 to us preaching together this year, I've never been so grateful for anything in my life as I have been for you. My greatest friend, my greatest advocate and my greatest source of love – how could I ever thank you for your heart in my every day? Nothing on this planet would have had any colour if you hadn't shown me the rainbows of God's light using you as a spectrum. Thank you for reminding me to never settle for the sake of settling, even if it means your grandchildren will come a little later – you'll get them in time. And they'll be worth the wait.

To my father, Revd Dr John Lloyd, in whom I found my passion. You have been my inspiration, my hero, my love and my teacher. Without you I'd never have found the courage to fight the good fight. From us dancing Michael

Acknowledgements

Flatley's *Riverdance* with unknown company in the elevator of a Parisian hotel, to your powerful sermons from the pulpit. For our leather-clad bike rides around those country lanes. For your vision for me in my life. The day before my eighteenth birthday you wrote me a letter saying I had two options in life: to use my skills for myself, or to use them for the benefit of others and therefore for God. This book hopefully proves I'm doing the latter.

You said it was just time that would separate you, Mum and me. Although I've loved the life God's given me, I can't wait to see you again, when I finally make it home.

Finally, face in the carpet adoration to my Deus, my Pater, my greatest storyteller, my joy, my everything, the one I'm utterly and totally besotted by, head over Louboutin heels in love with. Only you, Lord, know the details, know the journey, know the laughter, know the tears, know the fight. How can my soul thank you for all you've done for me? How can I ever repay you for the trials you helped me overcome? How did something so simple as love come from something as complex and as mysterious as you? Let's not let the end of this book be the end of our co-creations, for you're the best partner and the best creative director I've ever wished to spend all my time with. You reminded me of the stories I buried away in shame, while you were happy to polish them up and use them all over again.

Thank you for my life, my friends, my loves, for love itself, for those moments where your home invades our earth. Without your encounters, without your wisdom, I'd not be here – writing this for you.

This book is published by

Authentic Media

Find out more about us and our authors from our
website or Facebook page

authenticmedia.co.uk

facebook.com/authenticmedia

For more about Carrie, visit her blog:
herglassslipper.co.uk